Withdrawn

AIR

# Titles in the series

## AIR:
Green Science
Projects for a
Sustainable Planet
ISBN 978-0-7660-3646-8

## RECYCLE:
Green Science
Projects for a
Sustainable Planet
ISBN 978-0-7660-3648-2

## EARTH'S CYCLES:
Green Science Projects
About the Water Cycle,
Photosynthesis, and More
ISBN 978-0-7660-3643-7

## SOIL:
Green Science
Projects for a
Sustainable Planet
ISBN 978-0-7660-3647-5

## ENERGY:
Green Science Projects
About Solar, Wind,
and Water Power
ISBN 978-0-7660-3643-7

## WATER:
Green Science
Projects for a
Sustainable Planet
ISBN 978-0-7660-3645-1

# AIR

TEAM GREEN
SCIENCE PROJECTS

# GREEN
# SCIENCE
# PROJECTS
## FOR A
# SUSTAINABLE
# PLANET

**Robert Gardner**

**Enslow Publishers, Inc.**
40 Industrial Road
Box 398
Berkeley Heights, NJ 07922
USA

http://www.enslow.com

# AIR

## GREEN Science Projects for a Sustainable PLANET

**Library of Congress Cataloging-in-Publication Data**

Gardner, Robert, 1929–
    Air : green science projects for a sustainable planet / Robert Gardner.
        p. cm. — (Team green science projects)
    Includes bibliographical references and index.
    Summary: "Provides environmentally friendly 'green' science projects about air"—Provided
        by publisher.
    ISBN 978-0-7660-3646-8
    1. Air quality—Juvenile literature. 2. Air—Pollution—Juvenile literature. 3. Environmental
        quality—Juvenile literature. I. Title.
    TD883.G37 2011
    551.5078—dc22

                                                                2010001120

Printed in the United States of America

112010 Lake Book Manufacturing, Inc., Melrose Park, IL

10 9 8 7 6 5 4 3 2 1

**To Our Readers:** We have done our best to make sure all Internet Addresses in this book were
active and appropriate when we went to press. However, the author and the publisher have no
control over and assume no liability for the material available on those Internet sites or on other Web
sites they may link to. Any comments or suggestions can be sent by e-mail to comments@enslow.
com or to the address on the back cover.

♻ Enslow Publishers, Inc., is committed to printing our books on recycled paper. The paper in every
book contains 10% to 30% post-consumer waste (PCW). The cover board on the outside of each
book contains 100% PCW. Our goal is to do our part to help young people and the environment too!

**Illustration Credits:** Enslow Publishers, Inc., p. 44 (b);  Stephen Rountree (http://www.stephen
rountree.com), pp. 17, 26, 29, 52, 64, 68, 82, 91, 104, 113, 117; Tom LaBaff, p. 59 (a); Tom LaBaff
and Stephanie LaBaff, pp. 33, 41, 44 (a), 59 (b and c).

**Photo Credits:** Courtesy of Robert Gardner, p. 74; © iStockphoto.com: Justin Horrocks, p. 3,
monkeybusinessimages, p. 123, PhotoTalk, p. 11; John V. A. F. Neal/Photo Researchers, Inc.,
p. 54; Shutterstock.com, pp. 7, 8, 14, 49, 51, 53, 72, 76, 78, 83, 85, 95, 101, 109, 114.

**Cover Photo:** © Justin Horrocks/iStockphoto.com

# Contents

✅ Indicates experiments that offer ideas for science fair projects.

Indicates experiments that offer ideas for science fair projects.

# Introduction

We live under a sea—a sea of air much deeper than any ocean. We live at the bottom of this sea, where we enjoy crystal-clear blue skies, red sunsets, rainbows, halos, fluffy white clouds, cool breezes, falling snowflakes, and frost-covered grass. But it is here, too, that air polluted by smog and smoke casts an ugly film over the sky.

One-fifth of the air that makes up our atmosphere is oxygen, a gas we need to live. Air also contains carbon dioxide ($CO_2$), a gas that green plants absorb and use to make food. We release that same gas as a waste product in the air we exhale. When plants make food by a process known as photosynthesis, they release oxygen into the air.

In this book, you will learn about air, the gasses that make up air, and the gases and other matter that contaminate air. You will do so by reading, doing experiments to test a hypothesis, making models to illustrate ideas, carrying out demonstrations to better understand concepts, or making measurements. You will investigate air's properties and learn how it is being polluted. You will discover, too, what can be done to improve air quality and reduce global warming. You will also investigate ways to make air greener. By "green" we mean a way that doesn't harm the environment.

At times, as you do the experiments, demonstrations, and other activities, you may need a partner to help you. It is best to work with someone who enjoys experimenting as much as you do. That way, you will both enjoy what you are doing. **If any safety issue or danger is involved in doing an experiment, you will be warned. In some cases, to avoid danger you will be asked to work with an adult. Please do so.** We don't want you to take any chances that could lead to an injury.

# The Scientific Method

**S**cientists look at the world and try to understand how things work. They make careful observations and conduct research. Different areas of science use different approaches. Depending on the problem, one method is likely to be better than another. Designing a new medicine for heart disease, studying the spread of an invasive plant, such as purple loosestrife, and finding evidence of water on Mars require different methods.

Despite the differences, all scientists use a similar general approach in doing experiments. It is called the scientific method. In most experiments, some or all of the following steps are used: making an observation, formulating a question, making a hypothesis (an answer to the question) and a prediction (an if-then statement), designing and conducting an experiment, analyzing results, drawing conclusions, and accepting or rejecting the hypothesis. Scientists then share their findings by writing articles that are published in journals.

You might wonder how to start an experiment. When you observe something in the world, you may become curious and ask a question. Your question may be answered by a well-designed investigation. Once you have a question, you can make a hypothesis. Your hypothesis is a possible answer to the question. Once you have a hypothesis, it is time to design an experiment that will test your hypothesis.

In most cases, you should do a controlled experiment. This means having two groups that are treated the same except for the one factor being tested. That factor is called the variable. For example, suppose your question is, "Do green plants need carbon dioxide to live?" Your hypothesis might be that green plants do need carbon dioxide. You would use two groups of plants. One group, called the control group, would be placed in air that contains carbon dioxide. The other group, called the experimental group, would be placed in air that does not contain carbon dioxide. Both groups would be treated the same except for carbon dioxide. All plants would be planted in identical soil, receive the same amount of water and light, be kept at the same temperature, and so forth. Carbon dioxide would be the variable, the only difference between the two groups.

During the experiment, you would collect data about the plants: their growth, appearance, and so forth. By comparing the data collected from the control and experimental groups over time, you may be able to reach a conclusion.

# Science Fairs

Some of the investigations in this book contain ideas that may lead you to a science fair project. Those project ideas are indicated with a symbol ( ✅ ). However, judges at science fairs do not reward projects or experiments that are simply copied from a book. For example, a fluffy cotton model of a cloud would not impress most judges; however, a unique experiment to measure the concentration of atmospheric carbon dioxide would probably get their attention.

Science fair judges reward creative thought and imagination. It is difficult to be creative or imaginative unless you are really interested in your project. So try to choose an investigation that excites you. And before you jump into a project, consider your own talents and the cost of the materials you will need.

If you use an experiment or idea from this book for a science fair, find ways to modify or extend it. This should not be difficult. As you carry out investigations, new ideas will come to mind. You will think of questions that experiments can answer. The experiments will make excellent science fair projects, particularly because the ideas are your own and are interesting to you.

If you decide to enter a science fair and have never done so, read some of the books listed in the Further Reading section. Some of these books deal specifically with science fairs. They provide plenty of helpful hints and useful information. The books will help you avoid the pitfalls that sometimes plague first-time entrants. You will learn how to prepare appealing reports that include charts and graphs, set up and display your work, present your project, and relate to judges and visitors.

# Your Notebook

Like any good scientist, you will find it useful to record your ideas, notes, data, and conclusions in a notebook. By doing so, you will be able to refer to things you have done. It will also help you in doing future projects. Your notebook should contain ideas you may have as you experiment, sketches you draw, calculations you make, and hypotheses you may suggest. It should include a description of every experiment you do, the data you record, and so on. It should also contain the results of your experiments, calculations, graphs you draw, and any conclusions you may be able to reach based on your results.

# Safety First

As with many activities, safety is important in science. Certain rules apply when doing experiments. Some of the rules below may seem obvious to you, but it is important that you follow all of them.

1. Have **an adult** help you whenever the book advises.

2. Wear eye protection and closed-toe shoes (not sandals). Tie back long hair.

3. Do not eat or drink while experimenting. Never taste substances being used (unless instructed to do so).

4. Do not touch chemicals.

5. The liquid in some thermometers is mercury (a dense liquid metal). It is dangerous to touch mercury or breathe mercury vapor, and such thermometers have been banned in many states. When doing these experiments, use only non-mercury thermometers, such as those filled with alcohol. If you have a mercury thermometer in the house, **ask an adult** if it can be taken to a local thermometer exchange location.

6. Do only those experiments that are described in the book or those that have been approved by **an adult**.

7. Maintain a serious attitude while conducting experiments. Never engage in horseplay or play practical jokes.

8. Before beginning an experiment, read all of the instructions carefully and be sure you understand them.

9. Remove all items not needed for the experiment from your work space.

10. At the end of every activity, clean all materials used and put them away. Then wash your hands thoroughly with soap and water.

# Earth's Sea of Air

Unlike seas of water, the sea of air we live in can't be seen. Air is invisible and colorless. It has no odor so you can't smell it, and it is very light so you don't usually feel it. Because you do not usually notice the air around you, you may find it difficult to believe that we live in a sea of air. However, you become aware of air when you stand facing a strong wind. What you feel pushing against you is moving air. You have probably also felt wind when you rode your bike at a fast speed or when you ran swiftly during a game or a race. To make air more real to you, you can do an experiment.

# 1.1 The Reality of Air
## (An Experiment)

Things **YOU** will **Need:**

- ☑ large, plastic bag
- ☑ twist tie
- ☑ paper towels or napkins
- ☑ clear drinking glass
- ☑ dishpan
- ☑ tap water
- ☑ food coloring

Matter has mass and occupies space. Let's make a hypothesis: If air is matter, it must occupy space. So, a glass that appears to be empty must be filled with invisible air. If we let the air out of the glass under water, water should fill the space the air had occupied. Now, let's do an experiment to see if air really does occupy space.

1. Open a large, plastic bag. Hold it open and drag it through the air. Then seal it shut with a twist tie. You can't see anything in the bag. But do you feel something when you squeeze the bag?

2. Stuff a paper towel or napkin into the bottom of a clear drinking glass (Figure 1a). Turn the glass upside down. If the paper falls out, make it fit tighter.

3. Nearly fill a dishpan with tap water. Add a few drops of food coloring to make the water more visible.

# Figure 1

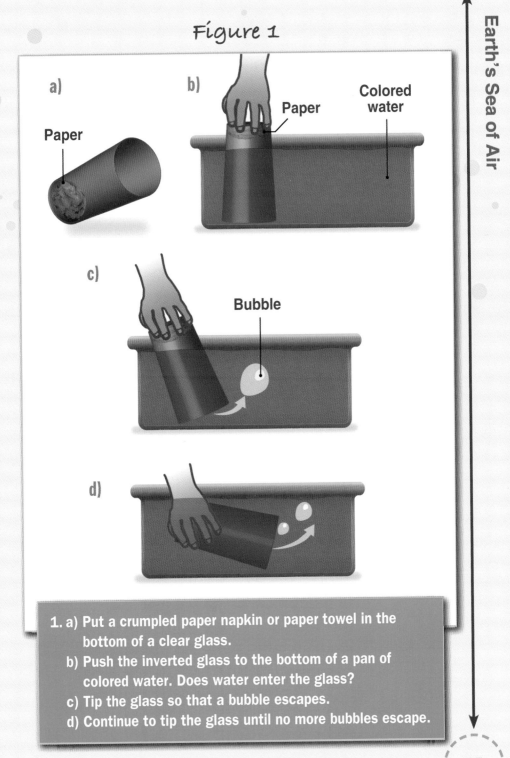

a) Paper

b) Paper — Colored water

c) Bubble

d)

1. a) Put a crumpled paper napkin or paper towel in the bottom of a clear glass.
   b) Push the inverted glass to the bottom of a pan of colored water. Does water enter the glass?
   c) Tip the glass so that a bubble escapes.
   d) Continue to tip the glass until no more bubbles escape.

4. Put the upside down glass into the colored water. Push it to the bottom of the water (Figure 1b). Does water go into the glass?

5. Lift the glass out of the water. Turn it right side up and take out the paper. Is the paper still dry?

6. Replace the paper and repeat step 4.

7. Slowly tip the glass until a bubble escapes from the glass (Figure 1c). What do you think the bubble was made of? Did any water replace the space the bubble occupied?

8. Slowly tip the glass so more bubbles escape. Does water replace the space the bubbles occupied? Continue to tip the glass until no more bubbles escape (Figure 1d).

9. Remove the glass from the water. Then remove the paper. Is the paper wet?

What evidence do you have to support the hypothesis that air occupies space?

## Mass and Weight

Mass and weight are not the same. The mass of an object is the amount of matter it contains. The weight of the same object is the force with which gravity pulls it toward the earth. Suppose an object is placed on one pan of an equal-arm balance. If it is balanced by a mass of one kilogram (2.2 lbs) on the opposite pan of the balance, we say its mass is 1.0 kg. Suppose the same mass is then hung from a spring balance. The spring will be stretched by a force equal to its weight (the force gravity exerts on it). That force is nearly 10 newtons (N) (2.2 lbs).

Now, imagine we take the 1.0 kg mass to the moon. The moon's gravity is only about one-sixth as strong as Earth's. When placed on a spring balance, the spring will only stretch one-sixth as much as it does on Earth. Its weight is much less—about 1.7 N. But, when placed on an equal arm balance, the 1.0 kg mass will still be balanced by a mass of 1.0 kg on the other balance pan. Its mass is still 1.0 kg; it is still the same amount of matter.

Sometimes when we weigh things on Earth, a weight may be expressed in grams or kilograms instead of newtons or pounds (the units of force or weight). It may be understood that it is really a weight and not a mass.

## Composition of Earth's Atmosphere

Our atmosphere covers Earth with a "blanket" of air more than 100 kilometers (60 mi) thick. Compared to Earth's radius of 6,380 kilometers (3,960 mi),

100 kilometers is a relatively thin blanket of air. It is only 1.5 percent as thick as Earth's radius, but it contains all the oxygen we breathe and all the moisture that falls as rain.

Air is a mixture of gases. A detailed list of the gases found in air is shown in Table 1.

As much as 5 percent of air is made up of water vapor. The amount of water in air varies greatly from day to day and place to place. For that reason, the table shows the composition of dry air—air from which all the gaseous water has been removed. In addition to varying amounts of water vapor, air also contains

| Table 1: Composition of Dry Air | | | |
|---|---|---|---|
| Gas | Chemical Formula | Percent by Volume* | Molecular Mass (amu)** |
| nitrogen | $N_2$ | 78.09 | 28 |
| oxygen | $O_2$ | 20.95 | 32 |
| argon | Ar | 0.93 | 39.9 |
| carbon dioxide | $CO_2$ | 0.039 | 44 |
| neon | Ne | 0.0018 | 20.2 |
| helium | He | 0.00052 | 4 |
| krypton | Kr | 0.0001 | 83.8 |
| hydrogen | $H_2$ | 0.00005 | 2 |
| xenon | Xe | 0.000008 | 131.3 |

* Total exceeds 100 because numbers have been rounded.
** The relative mass of the molecule compared to a carbon atom having a mass of 12 amu.

traces of other gases. These gases include ozone ($O_3$), carbon monoxide (CO), sulfur dioxide ($SO_2$), and radon (Rn).

Argon, neon, helium, krypton, xenon, and radon are gaseous elements called noble, or rare, gases. Argon, which is used in lightbulbs, is the only noble gas to make up a significant part of the atmosphere. Helium, as you know, is used in balloons and blimps. Neon and krypton are used to make colored light in electric signs. Radon is a harmful radioactive gas. It sometimes collects in buildings, especially in basement air. It comes from the decay of uranium compounds found under the ground. Radon can cause lung cancer, but its presence can be easily detected. Kits to measure radon are available at hardware stores, as are methods for removing it.

Carbon dioxide ($CO_2$), ozone, carbon monoxide, and dioxides of nitrogen and sulfur make up only a small fraction of our atmosphere. However, they are major air pollutants. Carbon dioxide and sulfur dioxide are produced when fossil fuels, such as coal and oil, burn. They combine with water in the air to form carbonic and sulfuric acids, which fall as acid rain on many parts of the world. Acid rain can harm trees, plants, and buildings. Sulfur dioxide can also be dangerous in dry air. It can cause breathing problems in people who have inhaled the gas.

Carbon dioxide is a serious concern to those seeking a greener world. The gas makes up only 0.039 percent of our atmosphere. This means that there are 390 molecules of carbon dioxide per one million molecules of air. Oxygen molecules are much more abundant at 210,000 parts per million (ppm).

While carbon dioxide makes up only a relatively small percentage of today's atmosphere, the amount of carbon dioxide in the air has increased by 23 percent since 1958 when it was 316 ppm and by 39 percent before the Industrial Revolution when it was 280 ppm.

## Greenhouse Gases and Global Warming

Carbon dioxide is a greenhouse gas. Like all greenhouse gases, it reflects heat back to the earth. As the amount of carbon dioxide in our atmosphere increases, more heat is trapped in Earth's atmosphere. The growing amount of carbon dioxide in the atmosphere is a major cause of global warming.

However, another gas, methane ($CH_4$), could become a greater threat. Methane is about 25 times as effective as carbon dioxide in trapping heat. Its present concentration in the air is very small. But huge amounts of methane and carbon dioxide are trapped in the frozen permafrost of the Arctic. Rising temperatures caused by global warming might cause the permafrost frozen in to melt, releasing the trapped gas. Between one-third and one-half of Arctic permafrost is already within 1.5°C (2.7°F) of its melting temperature.

Were this permafrost to melt, the concentration of carbon-containing gases in the air would increase greatly. Global warming could accelerate to as much as 0.32°C (0.58°F) per year by 2100. Glaciers would melt, causing oceans to rise and land to shrink. Weather patterns and ocean currents would change, causing huge climate changes.

Still another potent heat-trapping gas of growing importance is nitrogen trifluoride ($NF_3$). It is used in making microchips and flat-screen TVs. Its molecules linger for 550 years in the air. As a greenhouse gas, it is much more effective than carbon dioxide in trapping heat. Its present atmospheric concentration is only 0.04 percent that of carbon dioxide. However, its concentration is growing by about 11 percent per year. If its use in manufacturing increases, it could become a serious contributor to global warming.

Global warming is already having an impact on people, especially those with allergies. Increased levels of carbon dioxide have increased the growth of ragweed and have raised its production of pollen. To compound the matter, the pollen seems to be more potent, causing increased suffering among those allergic to ragweed pollen.

The effect is not limited to ragweed. Many species of trees are also producing more pollen. This may explain, in part, an increase in the number of people suffering from asthma. Increased carbon dioxide may also be responsible for the more widespread growth of poison ivy and its more potent rash-causing oil.

A warming globe is also responsible for the spreading of some animal species' normal habitats. In Alaska, where temperatures are rising faster than elsewhere, the number of insects that sting, such as bees and wasps, has increased. For Alaskans allergic to stings, this is bad news.

Carbon monoxide (CO) is produced by gasoline-burning engines in motor vehicles and by burning cigarettes. It combines with a chemical (hemoglobin) in our red blood cells. When it does, the hemoglobin can no longer combine with oxygen to carry it from our lungs to the rest of our bodies. Carbon monoxide can increase to dangerous levels in heavy traffic and stagnant air. Breathing a heavy concentration of carbon monoxide can be fatal. For that reason, every home should have a carbon monoxide detector. These devices will sound an alarm when carbon monoxide levels become dangerous.

Close to Earth's surface, ozone makes up part of the smog found in some large cities. Bright sunlight and exhaust fumes from motor vehicles combine to create smog. The ozone in smog can be very irritating to your eyes.

## Ozone in the Stratosphere

The ozone in smog is also found in the stratosphere, which extends from about 13 to 50 kilometers (8 to 31 mi) above Earth's surface. This ozone, high above the earth, plays a valuable role in protecting us from the sun's ultraviolet light. Ozone absorbs some of the ultraviolet light coming from the sun. Without the stratosphere's ozone layer, much more ultraviolet light would reach Earth's surface. Ultraviolet light damages living cells. It is sometimes used to destroy harmful bacteria. However, it can also damage skin cells and cause skin cancer.

The amount of ozone in the upper atmosphere has decreased because of chlorofluorocarbons (CFCs), such as Freon gas. The gas was once used in spray cans, air conditioners, and some solvents. Freon slowly spread into the stratosphere where it decomposed, releasing chlorine. Chlorine reacts with ozone, producing oxygen and chlorine oxide, gases that do not absorb much ultraviolet light. For this reason, Freon is no longer made in the United States. The banning of chlorofluorocarbons has increased the amount of ozone in the stratosphere and lessened the threat of skin cancer. But CFC molecules have a long life span—100 years or more. It may be decades before the level of ozone in the stratosphere returns to normal.

Beware that ultraviolet light is used in tanning beds. It is just as dangerous there as it is in sunlight.

# Air Pressure

Pressure is defined as force divided by the area on which the force acts. When you stand on the ground there is a pressure on your feet. Your weight provides the force; the area is the area of your feet on which your weight rests. Suppose you weigh 100 pounds and the area of each of your feet is 40 square inches. The pressure on your feet is:

$$\frac{100 \text{ lb}}{2 \times 40 \text{ in}^2} = 1.25 \text{ lb/in}^2.$$

If air has weight, it must push against Earth's surface causing pressure. Can we detect that air pressure? If we can, can it be measured?

# Measuring Air Pressure

You may have detected changes in air pressure when you ascended or descended in an airplane or in an elevator. You could feel pressure changes in your ears.

An instrument to measure air pressure was invented in 1643 by Italian physicist Evangelista Torricelli (1608–1647). The instrument is called a

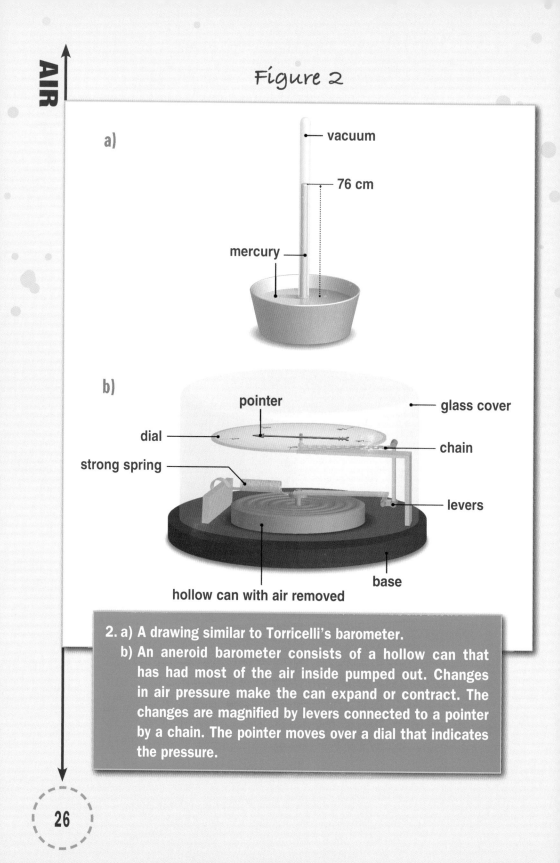

# Figure 2

a)

vacuum

76 cm

mercury

b)

pointer

glass cover

dial

chain

strong spring

levers

hollow can with air removed

base

2. a) A drawing similar to Torricelli's barometer.
   b) An aneroid barometer consists of a hollow can that has had most of the air inside pumped out. Changes in air pressure make the can expand or contract. The changes are magnified by levers connected to a pointer by a chain. The pointer moves over a dial that indicates the pressure.

barometer. Torricelli's barometer consisted of a 1.2-meter (4-ft)-long glass tube that he filled with mercury. With one end of the tube sealed and the other plugged with his thumb, Torricelli inverted the device and placed the open end of the tube in a dish of mercury. The mercury then began to empty into the dish. But it stopped when the level of mercury in the tube was 76 centimeters (30 in) above the mercury in the dish (Figure 2a). This left an empty space at the top of the tube. Torricelli reasoned that the empty space was a vacuum because no air bubbles had gone up the tube. He realized that the weight of the mercury pushing down at the mouth of the tube was balanced by the pressure of the air pushing upward. (Air exerts pressure in all directions: up, down, and sideways.)

Air pressure is still often measured by the height of mercury in a barometer similar to Torricelli's. Normal air pressure at sea level will balance a column of mercury 76 centimeters (30 in) high. Air pressure may be expressed in millibars. Normal air pressure at sea level is 1,030 millibars.

Mercury is expensive and its vapors are poisonous. Therefore, you should measure air pressure with an aneroid barometer like the one shown in Figure 2b. It contains no mercury. But before you experiment with an aneroid barometer, let's first understand how it works and find out how air can be weighed.

# 1.2 How Does an Aneroid Barometer Work? (A Demonstration)

**Things YOU will Need:**

- scissors
- large balloon
- wide-mouth drinking glass
- strong rubber band
- 2 drinking straws
- tape
- cardboard
- clothespin
- ruler
- marking pen
- place where temperature remains relatively constant
- pen or pencil
- notebook
- changing weather
- commercial aneroid barometer

Figure 2 showed how an aneroid barometer works. But the series of levers make it difficult to see how changes in air pressure can move the pointer over the dial. This demonstration will show how changes in air pressure can move a pointer.

# Figure 3

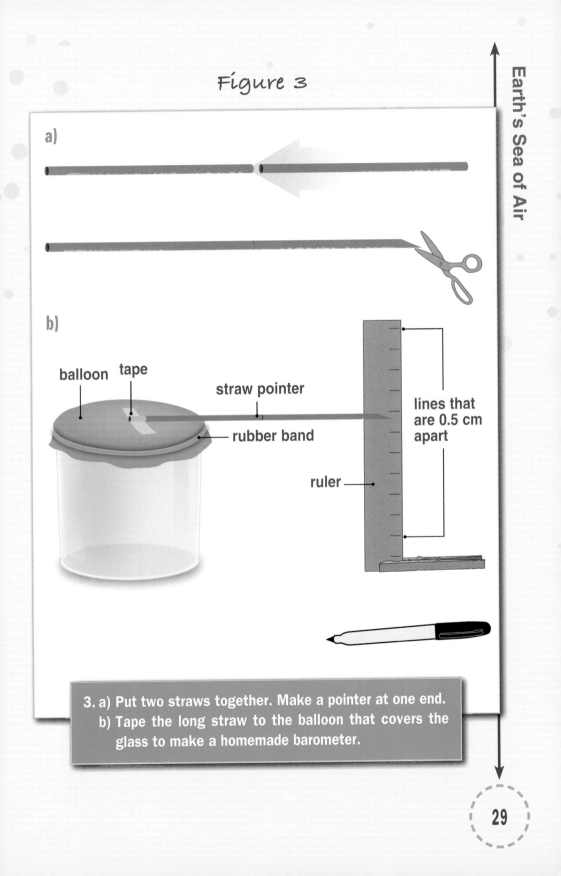

a)

b)

balloon    tape

straw pointer

rubber band

lines that
are 0.5 cm
apart

ruler

3. a) Put two straws together. Make a pointer at one end.
   b) Tape the long straw to the balloon that covers the glass to make a homemade barometer.

1. Use scissors to cut off the neck of a balloon.

2. Pull the remaining part of the balloon over the top of a wide-mouth drinking glass. Fasten it to the glass with a strong rubber band.

3. To put two drinking straws together, squeeze the end of one and slide it into the other. Make one end of the straws into a pointer (Figure 3a) by cutting that end diagonally with scissors.

4. Tape the other end of the pointer to the center of the rubber balloon covering the glass.

5. Make a scale using cardboard, a clothespin, a ruler, and a marking pen as shown in Figure 3b.

6. Put your homemade barometer in a place where the temperature remains relatively constant, such as a basement. Why should the temperature be constant? Hint: The working part of this barometer contains air.

7. Record the position of the pointer in your notebook. Record the position of the pointer every few hours for the next few days. Be sure to note when the weather is changing from fair to stormy or vice versa.

8. Compare the readings from your homemade barometer with those of a commercial aneroid barometer. How does the homemade barometer indicate increasing air pressure? Decreasing air pressure? How is your homemade barometer like a real aneroid barometer? How is it different?

## Ideas for Science Fair Projects

- Design and carry out an experiment to show how the volume of air is affected by temperature.

- Design and carry out an experiment to show how the volume of air is affected by pressure.

# 1.3 Weighing Air
## (An Experiment)

**Things YOU will Need:**
- ☑ large, clear plastic bag
- ☑ twist tie
- ☑ balance that can weigh to $\pm 0.1$ g

*Hypothesis: Since air occupies space, we should be able to weigh it.*

1. Weigh a large, clear plastic bag and a twist tie.

2. Fill the bag with air by holding it open as you drag it through the air.

3. Seal the bag of air with the same twist tie you weighed with the bag.

4. Place the bag of air on a balance. How does the weight of the air-filled bag compare with the weight of the empty bag and twist tie?

You probably found that the air had no weight. How can that be? Is the hypothesis wrong?

If air is matter it should have mass. To see why the air appeared to have no mass, you can do another experiment.

# 1.4 Archimedes, Air, and Buoyancy
## (An Experiment)

**Things YOU will Need:**

- clay
- string
- spring scale
- notebook
- pen or pencil
- cold water
- bucket
- metric measuring cup
- platform balance that can weigh to $\pm 0.1$ g

The reason air has no weight when weighed in air was explained long ago by the Greek scientist Archimedes. To see what Archimedes discovered, you can do an experiment similar to his.

1. Form a large ball of clay about 5 centimeters (2 in) in diameter around one end of a length of string.

2. Make a loop at the free end of the string. Hang the clay ball on a spring scale as shown in Figure 4a. How much does the clay weigh? Record its weight in your notebook.

3. Submerge the clay in a bucket of water and weigh it again, as shown in Figure 4b. Record its weight in water. How much weight did the clay appear to lose in water? (Save the clay for the next step.)

How do you think your weight in water would compare with your weight in air? If you can float in water, what would you weigh in water?

# Figure 4

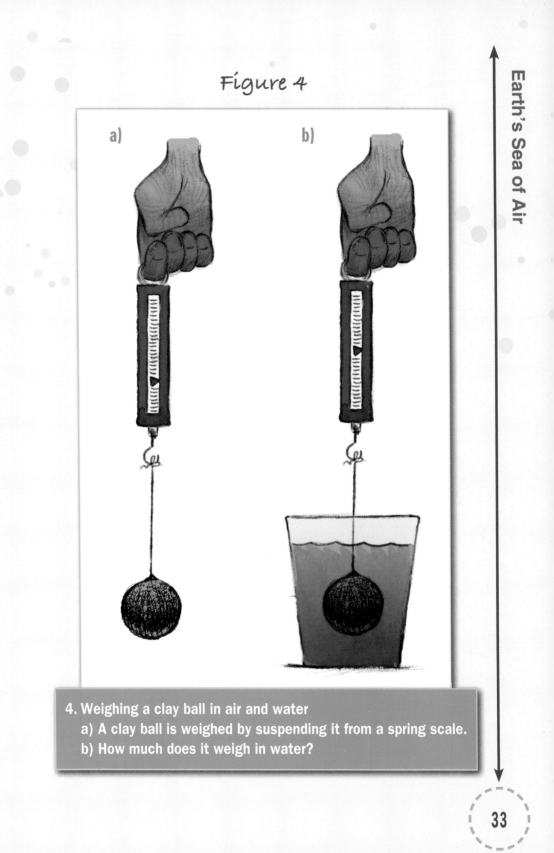

a)

b)

4. Weighing a clay ball in air and water
   a) A clay ball is weighed by suspending it from a spring scale.
   b) How much does it weigh in water?

**4.** Hang the clay ball in a metric measuring cup half filled with water. What volume of water does it displace? What is the volume of the clay? Record the clay ball's volume.

**5.** What is the weight of the water displaced by the clay? To find the weight of the volume of water displaced by the clay we can measure the density of water. The density is weight or mass divided by volume. For example, the density of air is about 1.2 grams per liter or 0.0012 g/mL. The density of iron is 7.9 g/cm³. [A cubic centimeter (cm³) and a milliliter (mL) are the same volume.]

**6.** To find the density of water, weigh a dry, empty graduated cylinder or metric measuring cup on a balance. Record its weight.

**7.** Add cold water to the measuring cup or cylinder until the water reaches the top measuring line.

**8.** Reweigh the cup or cylinder now that it is filled with water. Record that weight. How can you find the weight of the water alone?

**9.** What is the density of the water? For example, suppose your data table is similar to the one below.

| Mass of Cup | Volume of Water Added | Mass of Water and Cup |
|---|---|---|
| 9.0 g | 100 mL | 109.0 g |

You conclude that the water's mass was 100 g because

$$109.0 \text{ g} - 9.0 \text{ g} = 100.0 \text{g.}$$

The density of the water is its weight (100 g) divided by its volume (100 mL).

Therefore, the density of the water is:

$$\text{density} = \frac{\text{weight}}{\text{volume}} = \frac{100.0 \text{ g}}{100 \text{ mL}} = 1.0 \text{ g/mL.}$$

You probably found the density of water to be 1.0 g/mL or very nearly so.

How much weight did the clay appear to lose when weighed in water? How does the clay's loss of weight in water compare with the weight of the water it displaces?

You and Archimedes would probably agree that *an object submerged in a fluid is buoyed (pushed) up by a force equal to the weight of the fluid it displaces.*

Archimedes' principle, stated above, is not limited to water. It says, "buoyed up by the weight of *the fluid it displaces.*" His principle works with any fluid—liquid *or* gas.

Since Archimedes' principle applies to gases, why does air weighed in air have no weight?

## Ideas for Science Fair Projects

- Repeat the above demonstration several times using different solids. You might try a bunch of steel washers held together with thread, a stack of coins held together with tape, or lead sinkers with different volumes. Are your results similar in each case? As accurately as your measurements allow, does a solid's loss of weight in water always equal the weight of the water displaced?

- The density of air at room temperature is about 1.2 grams per liter. How can you confirm this density by applying Archimedes' principle to an air-filled balloon weighed on a balance?

- Design an experiment to determine your weight while submerged in water. Then, under adult supervision, carry out your experiment.

- Why are very accurate measurements of mass done in a vacuum?

- Place an egg in a pint-size jar that is nearly filled with water. The egg sinks. Add a heaping tablespoonful of salt to the water and stir. Why does the egg now float? Can you find a way to make the egg float in the *middle* of the jar?

# Weighing Air

According to Archimedes' principle, any object is buoyed upward by a force equal to the weight of the fluid it displaces. Air weighed in air displaces air. It is buoyed upward by its own weight. Therefore, it appears to be weightless.

To accurately weigh air, or any gas, the air is first pumped out of a rigid container that can be sealed. The container, which now holds a vacuum, is weighed.

To fill the container with a gas, it is connected to a tube with a valve. This tube is also connected to a gas container. When the valve is opened, the gas flows into the empty container. In the case of air, the end of the tube can simply open to the air outside the evacuated container.

Once the container is filled with a gas, it can be resealed and weighed. The weight of the empty container is subtracted from this weight to find the weight of the gas.

Some data for a weighing of a container of air is shown below. As you can see, one liter (L) of air does not weigh very much. However, a room full of air might hold 100 kilograms (220 lbs) or more.

| Mass of Evacuated Container (g) | Volume of Container (mL) | Mass of Container + Air | Mass of Air (g) | Density of Air* (g/mL) g/L |
|---|---|---|---|---|
| 251.04 | 500 | 251.68 | 0.64 | 0.00128 1.28 |

**\* Remember density is mass divided by volume. In this experiment the density is 0.64 g/0.5 L = 1.28 g/L.**

# 1.5 An Aneroid Barometer, Air Pressure, and Altitude
## (An Experiment)

**Things YOU will Need:**

- an adult
- aneroid barometer
- notebook
- pen or pencil
- tall building or hill
- automobile
- airplane (optional)
- bag of potato chips

As we go up into the air, there is less air above us to push on us. So let's make a hypothesis: As we climb a hill or go up in a tall building, the air pressure will decrease.

Now, you can do an experiment to see if our hypothesis is correct.

1. Obtain an aneroid barometer like the one that was shown in Figure 2b. It will work as well inside a building as outside because no building is airtight.

2. Take your aneroid barometer to the basement of a building or the base of a hill. If possible, choose a tall building

or hill. A skyscraper or a mountain would be ideal. Smaller heights will work if you read the barometer carefully.

**3.** Read the barometer and record the air pressure.

**4.** Carry the barometer to the top floor of the building or top of the hill. Read the barometer carefully again. Record the air pressure. Do the results agree with the hypothesis?

**5.** Go for an automobile ride with **an adult** driver and take your aneroid barometer with you. Try to predict how the air pressure will change as you go up and down hills or mountains.

**6.** The next time you ride on an airplane, take along an unopened bag of potato chips. (Although airplane cabins are pressurized, your ears tell you that the pressure decreases as you ascend.) Feel the bag at low and high altitudes. What do you notice about the bag's firmness at different altitudes? How can you explain what you observe? What else could change the bag's firmness?

# Ideas for Science Fair Projects

- Measure air pressure at different altitudes. Plot a graph of air pressure versus altitude. How can you use air pressure to measure altitude?

- Design and carry out an experiment to show that the pressure exerted by air or water at a particular point is equal in all directions: up, down, and sideways.

- Would you expect there to be a relationship between the number of home runs hit and the altitude of a major league baseball field? Do some research to find out. Is there a relationship? What other factors should you consider?

- Build a barometer that uses water instead of mercury. How long a tube will you need to measure air pressure with such a barometer?

# Layers of Atmosphere

Early scientists did not know how high the atmosphere extends into space. But in 1648, Blaise Pascal (1623–1662) asked his brother-in-law to measure air pressure at various altitudes while climbing the Puy de Dôme Mountain in France. His results probably agreed with what you found in Experiment 1.6. The higher he climbed, the lower the air pressure.

When people began to ascend above Earth's surface in balloons, airplanes, rockets, and spaceships, Pascal's results were confirmed. Air pressure decreased all the way to the vacuum of outer space.

Figure 5 shows how meteorologists (scientists who study weather) divide our atmosphere into a series of layers. The troposphere, where most weather takes place, goes from Earth's surface to a height of about 13 kilometers (8 mi). (One mile is about 1.6 kilometers.) As we ascend into the troposphere, the temperature falls. The tropopause is the boundary between the troposphere and the stratosphere. Temperatures in the first few miles of the stratosphere remain constant at approximately –60°C (–76°F). But near the top of the stratosphere temperatures increase to about –5°C (23°F). The relatively warm upper stratosphere is due to the absorption of ultraviolet light by ozone molecules. Temperatures again diminish through the mesosphere only to rise again in the thermosphere at altitudes greater than 80 kilometers (50 mi).

Nearly all the air's weight is below a height of 100 kilometers (60 mi). As Figure 5 shows, air pressure at the tropopause is one-tenth the pressure at Earth's

## Figure 5

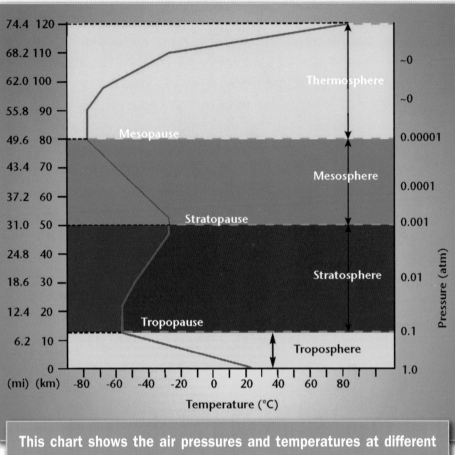

This chart shows the air pressures and temperatures at different altitudes within the layers of atmosphere above the earth.

surface. At the top of the stratosphere, air pressure is about one-thousandth its value at sea level.

It is in the troposphere that we see clouds. This is where weather happens. It is in this part of the atmosphere that raindrops and snowflakes form, winds blow, temperature and air pressure changes, and tornadoes, hurricanes, and thunderstorms are produced.

The "thinner" air at high altitudes makes it difficult to breathe. At the tops of peaks in the Rocky Mountains the altitude is about 3,700 meters (12,000 ft). The low air pressure on these mountains means that you take in less oxygen with each breath. You have to breathe faster to get the oxygen you need. Your heart must also beat faster to carry the reduced oxygen in your blood to the rest of your body.

With time, you can adjust to high altitude. You become *acclimatized*. Your body produces more red blood cells. The added cells allow more oxygen to move from your lungs to the cells of your body. You also learn to take deeper breaths so that more oxygen enters your lungs. The people who live in the Andes Mountains of South America are able to work at an altitude of 5,800 meters (19,000 ft) without ill effects. At this altitude, the air pressure and the concentration of oxygen are both less than half that at sea level. Blood tests show that these people have almost twice as many red blood cells as normal. Their lungs are also bigger and have more surface area. This makes it possible for more of the oxygen they breathe to get into their blood. Jet airplanes, which fly at high altitudes, pressurize the air inside the plane to prevent passengers from feeling sick or short of breath.

# 1.6 Having Fun With Air Pressure Effects
## (Demonstrations)

**A**ir pressure explains a number of startling effects that may, at first, seem like magic. You can enjoy these effects and show them to family and friends using these demonstrations.

## A Straw Pipette

1. Chemists use pipettes to move liquids from one container to another. You can make a pipette from a drinking straw. Lower a clear, plastic drinking straw into a glass of water.

# Figure 6

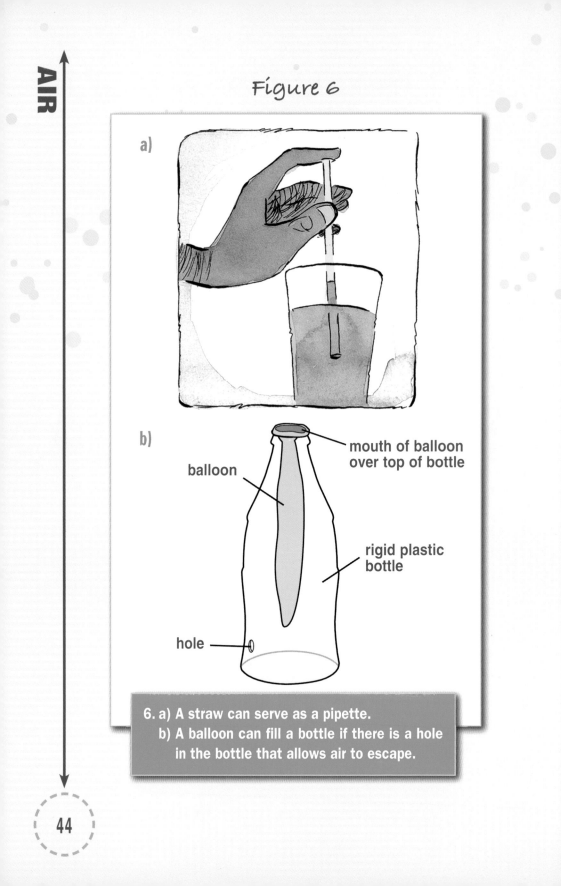

a)

b)

mouth of balloon
over top of bottle

balloon

rigid plastic
bottle

hole

6. a) A straw can serve as a pipette.
   b) A balloon can fill a bottle if there is a hole
   in the bottle that allows air to escape.

Place your index finger or thumb firmly on the top of the straw as shown in Figure 6a. Lift the straw. The water will remain in the straw. Hold your pipette over a sink. What happens when you remove your finger from the top of the straw?

2. Use another clear plastic straw to drink water from a glass. Use a finishing nail to make a hole through the straw about 5 centimeters (2 in) below its upper end. What happens when you try to drink through the straw now? Cover the hole with your finger. Can you drink through the straw if you cover the hole? What do you think will happen if you try to use this straw with a hole as a pipette? Try it! Were you right?

## What Happened?

When the water below your finger in the drinking straw pipette starts to fall from the straw, the air column below your finger slightly lengthens. The air above the water in the straw exerts less pressure than the air below the water, so the water stays in the straw. When you remove your finger, air enters the top of the straw. The air pressure above and below the water become equal. The water's weight then causes it to fall.

When you drink liquid through a straw, you draw air out of the straw. This reduces the air pressure inside the straw. As air pressure outside the straw becomes greater than the pressure in the straw, liquid is pushed up the straw to your mouth. If you make a hole near the top of the straw, air can enter the straw through the hole. The air pressure in the straw is now the same as the pressure outside. There is no force to push water up the straw.

# An Amazing Upside Down Bottle of Water

1. Fill a glass as full as possible with water.

2. Use scissors to cut a piece of thin, corrugated cardboard that is slightly larger than the mouth of the glass.

3. Wet the cardboard. Then put it on the mouth of the glass. Hold the cardboard against the top of the glass as you invert the glass over a sink. Remove your hand from the cardboard. The water should stay in the glass.

## What Happened?

Air pressure can support a column of mercury 76 centimeters (30 in) high and a column of water 10 meters (34 ft) tall, so it can easily support a column of water in a glass.

# A Sticky Funnel

1. Put a kitchen funnel into the mouth of a bottle. Pour some water into the funnel. Notice that the water runs freely through the funnel into the bottle.

2. Remove the funnel. Place a ring of soft clay around the mouth of the bottle. Put the funnel back on the bottle. Use the clay to create a seal so that air does not enter the bottle around the funnel. What happens now when you pour water into the funnel?

3. Find a paper clip and straighten it. Gently push the end of the paper clip through the clay to make a hole. What happens to the water in the funnel after you make the hole?

## What Happened?

When the funnel rests on the bottle's neck, air can escape from the flask as it is replaced by water pouring through the funnel. But when clay seals the connection between the funnel and the bottle, air cannot escape from the bottle. The water that passes through the funnel compresses the air in the bottle. The increased air pressure inside the bottle becomes equal to the pressure of the air and the water in the funnel. When the pressures are equal, water will not flow through the funnel. Making a hole in the clay allows air to leave the bottle so the water will flow.

# A Balloon in a Bottle

1. Find a plastic bottle that has a narrow neck, such as a liquid soap bottle.

2. Put the round part of a balloon inside the bottle and pull the mouth of the balloon over the top of the bottle.

3. Try to blow up the balloon. You will find that you can't add much air to the balloon.

4. Use a nail to make a small hole in the side of the bottle near the bottom. Do not make a hole in the balloon.

5. Now, try to blow up the balloon again. You can now inflate the balloon until it fills the bottle (Figure 6b).

6. Blow up the balloon until it fills the bottle once more. Keep the balloon inflated and place your finger firmly over the hole. Take your mouth away from the balloon. Why does the balloon continue to fill the bottle? What happens when you remove your finger?

## What Happened?

When you first tried to inflate the balloon, the growing balloon quickly compressed the air trapped in the bottle. The increased air pressure in the bottle made it impossible to blow up the balloon any further.

When put a hole in the bottle, you were able to inflate the balloon because air could escape from the bottle. By putting your finger over the hole, the balloon remained inflated. A small amount of air came out of the balloon. Then the air pressure around the balloon was less than the pressure inside the balloon. The balloon remained inflated because air could not enter the bottle.

## Air Pressure: A Real Crusher

This demonstration requires heat and hot objects so it should be done by **an adult** wearing safety glasses.

1. Nearly fill a small pail with cold water. Place it in the kitchen sink.

2. Rinse out the inside of an empty, 12-ounce aluminum soda can with water.

3. Use a metric measuring cup to pour 45 mL (1.5 oz) of cold water into the can. Leave the opening at the top of the can uncovered.

4. **Have the adult** use kitchen tongs to hold the can on a hot plate or stove burner. Allow the water to boil for about one minute so that steam replaces most of the air in the can.

5. **The adult** should continue to hold the can with tongs as he removes it from the heat, turns it upside down, and places the open end of the can in the pail of cold water. Bang! The can collapses with a loud THUMP!!

## What Happened?

The steam forced air from the can. When the steam-filled can was sealed and cooled by placing the open end in cold water, the steam quickly condensed (changed to water). When the steam changed to water, the pressure inside the can suddenly decreased because water takes up much less space than the gas (steam) from which it came. Meanwhile, the pressure of the air pushing on the outside of the can remained unchanged. Because the pressure on the outside of the can was suddenly much greater than the pressure on the inside, the can was crushed.

# Air, Buildings, Heating, and Energy

To stay warm during the winter, the air inside your home must be heated. This can be done in different ways. Some homes use a furnace that burns gas, fuel oil, coal, wood, or some other fuel to heat the air. A fan can then blow the warm air along ducts to openings in the floor or walls of the building. Other homes use a furnace to heat water that circulates through pipes to radiators, which warm the air in rooms. Another way to warm a home is by using electrical energy to generate heat in electrical resistors that warm the air.

The greenest way to warm the air inside buildings is to use the sun. Solar panels with photovoltaic cells on the roof of a building produce electrical energy. These cells change sunlight into electricity. Some or all of the electrical energy needed to heat the building can be generated by solar panels.

In the Northern Hemisphere, solar collectors can be placed on south-facing roofs. The solar collectors absorb light energy and change it to thermal (heat) energy. The heat can be used to provide hot water. It can also heat air or water that can be used to heat the building. Solar collectors have a black metal plate that absorbs solar energy. The warm plate transfers heat to a fluid (air or water) flowing over it. The fluid, circulated by a pump or a fan, carries the heat to the inside of

Photovoltaic cells on this roof can convert light energy into electrical energy.

Solar collectors can convert light energy into thermal energy that can be used to heat air or water.

the building. The collector is covered by two sheets of glass (Figure 7). The glass reflects heat emitted by the black plate. It acts like a miniature greenhouse, allowing little heat to escape to the outside air.

Of course, the sun does not shine at night and is often behind clouds. To make up for times of darkness and clouds, many solar systems store heat. Hot air may be circulated through a bin of rocks that absorb the air's heat. A tank to store hot water for household use may be embedded in the rocks. The heat may also be stored in large tanks of water. A backup system is often available for those times when the solar system cannot provide enough energy for

## Figure 7

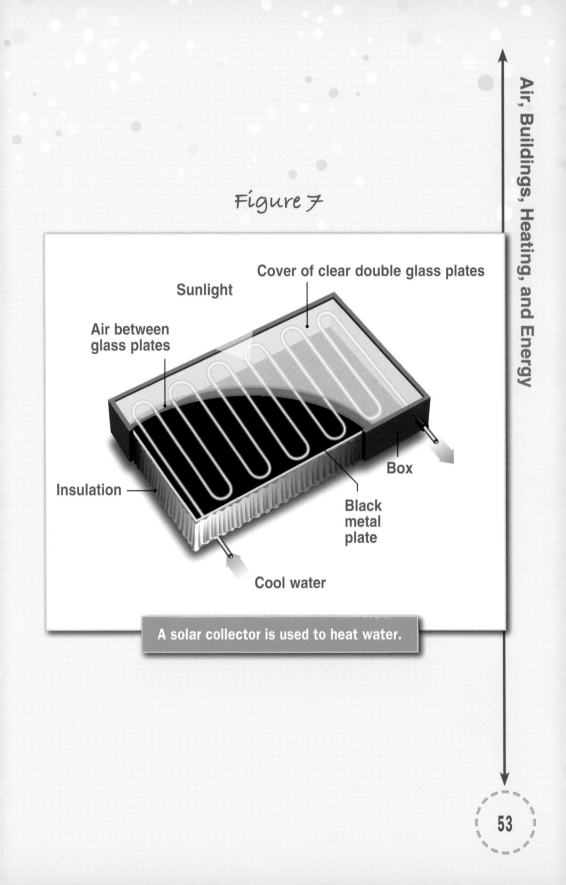

Sunlight

Cover of clear double glass plates

Air between glass plates

Insulation

Box

Black metal plate

Cool water

A solar collector is used to heat water.

the home. Backup systems typically use gas, oil, or electricity to provide heat.

Some buildings use a passive solar system. Such systems do not have solar panels or pumps to circulate hot air or water. Instead, the building has lots of south-facing windows that let in sunlight. Solar energy is absorbed and stored in dark concrete walls and floors or by tanks of water. At night, insulated shades cover the windows. The warm concrete or water radiates heat to warm the building's air.

This passive solar system uses sunlight to warm this home. At night the warm concrete radiates heat, keeping the air warm.

# 2.1 Light to Electricity
## (An Experiment)

*Hypothesis: A photovoltaic cell will produce electricity when exposed to light.*

**1.** On a sunny day, take the photovoltaic cell, wires, and ammeter outside.

**2.** Use the wires to connect the leads from the photovoltaic cell to the ammeter.

**3.** Place the photovoltaic cell in direct sunlight. What happens to the needle on the ammeter? If the needle moves the wrong way, reverse the connections to the ammeter. If the needle then goes off scale, cover part of the photovoltaic cell. Was the hypothesis correct?

**4.** How does the amount of photovoltaic cell surface exposed to the sun affect the electric current? Make a hypothesis. Then cover varying amounts of the photovoltaic cell's surface exposed to the sun. Was your hypothesis correct?

**5.** How will the angle at which the sun strikes the cell affect the electric current? Form a hypothesis. Then vary the angle at which the sunlight strikes the photovoltaic cell's surface. Was your hypothesis correct?

# 2.2 Sunlight to Heat: A Solar Collector to Heat Air (A Model)

**Things YOU will Need:**

- ✓ large, aluminum pie pan
- ✓ flat, black paint
- ✓ masking tape
- ✓ cardboard
- ✓ household thermometer (−10–50°C or 10–120°F)
- ✓ paintbrush
- ✓ notebook
- ✓ pen or pencil
- ✓ clear tape
- ✓ clear plastic wrap
- ✓ bright sunlight

You can make a model solar collector to show how energy from the sun can be used to heat air.

1. Paint the inside of a large aluminum pie pan with flat, black paint.

2. After the paint dries, tape the pan to a sheet of cardboard. The cardboard will help to insulate the pan.

3. Use a thermometer to determine the outside air temperature in the sun. Put the thermometer on the cardboard sheet. Shade the thermometer bulb with a small piece of cardboard folded like a tent. When the thermometer reading becomes steady, record the air temperature.

4. Put the thermometer with its shaded bulb in the black aluminum pan. Use a small piece of clear tape to fasten the thermometer and the "tent" to the pan.

5. Cover and seal the air in the pan with clear plastic wrap to represent the solar collector's glass cover.

6. Place the cardboard sheet with its model solar collector in bright sunlight.

7. Watch the thermometer. What happens to the temperature of the air in the solar collector? If the temperature gets close to the maximum the thermometer can measure, remove the collector from the sunlight.

What is the highest temperature you recorded? How does it compare with the air temperature?

## Ideas for Science Fair Projects

- To see how the black color affects a solar collector, find an identical unpainted pan. Repeat the experiment using the unpainted pan. What can you conclude?

- Make a model solar collector in which the heated air warms a model house.

# 2.3 Air and Heating
## (An Experiment)

Air is commonly used to move heat in a building. Form a hypothesis to explain how air moves heat. Then do this experiment.

1. Let's examine a property of air that is true of all gases. Obtain a clean, empty, 1-liter plastic soda bottle. Pull the neck of a balloon over the mouth of the bottle.

2. Hold the bottle in a pan of hot tap water (Figure 8a). What happens to the balloon? Why do you think the balloon expands?

3. Hold the bottle in a pan of cold water with a few ice cubes. What happens to the balloon? Explain what you observe.

   What happens to the density of air when it is heated? When it is cooled?

4. Use scissors to remove the bottom from a foam cup.

5. Use a small piece of clay to support a birthday candle on the bottom of the foam cup.

## Figure 8

8. a) A bottle of air topped with a balloon is placed in hot water. What happens?
   b) Mount a birthday candle on a small foam base. Lower a jar into the water over the burning candle. What happens?
   c) What happens to the warm fluid when it flows into the cold fluid?

6. Add some cold water to a pie pan. Float the birthday candle on the water.

7. **Ask an adult** to light the birthday candle. When it is burning steadily, slowly lower a tall plastic jar over the candle (Figure 8b). Watch what happens when the jar touches the water. Let the jar rest on the pan.

8. What happens to the water level in the jar after the candle goes out? Can you explain what you observe?

   Remember that liquids and gases are both fluids and behave in similar ways.

9. Nearly fill a clear vial with cold water. In a separate vial, add several drops of food coloring to some hot tap water. Watch the food coloring diffuse (spread out) into the water.

10. Use a medicine dropper to remove some of the hot, colored water.

11. Place the tip of the medicine dropper near the bottom of the vial of cold water. Slowly squeeze the dropper bulb to force the warm, colored water into the cold water (Figure 8c). What happens to the colored water? Can you explain what happens?

12. Now, reverse the experiment. Predict what will happen when you add colored cold water to a vial of clear hot water. Were you right?

13. **Ask an adult** to turn on a stove's heating element. Then have **the adult** hold a facial tissue well above the heat. What happens to the tissue? Which way is the hot air moving? Why do you think it is moving that way?

Do the results of this experiment support your hypothesis? If not, how would you change your hypothesis based on the results of this experiment?

# Insulating Air to Reduce Heat Loss (An Experiment)

Things
YOU will
Need:

**Things YOU will Need:**

- cardboard box about 30 centimeters (12 in) on a side
- light socket
- 15-watt incandescent lightbulb
- tape
- large nail
- digital or alcohol laboratory thermometer ($-10-110°C$)
- digital or alcohol household thermometer
- wall outlet
- clock or watch
- pen or pencil
- notebook
- large, insulated box or string and rigid-board insulation
- gloves

When it is cold outside, the air in a building has to be heated to keep its occupants warm and prevent water from freezing. To reduce heat loss and keep heating costs low, buildings should be well insulated. Insulating materials, such as chopped paper (cellulose) and fiberglass, reduce the rate at which heat travels from warm inside air to cold outside air. Insulating a building is a green action. It conserves energy because less fuel will be needed to warm the building's air.

To understand how insulation reduces the heat loss, imagine warm air molecules inside a building.

Like all molecules, air molecules (mostly nitrogen and oxygen) are constantly moving. They have kinetic (motion) energy. Temperature is a measure of the average kinetic energy of molecules. As the temperature increases, so does the molecules' kinetic energy. A building's thermal (heat) energy is the total kinetic energy of all the air molecules in the building.

The speedy air molecules inside a heated building bump into each other. They also bump into the walls. The molecules that make up the wall then bump into each other. If the walls are not well insulated, molecular collisions (bumps) will carry the air's thermal energy to slower-moving molecules in the cooler outside walls and outside air. As a result, heat moves from warm air inside a building to cooler air outside. To reduce the rate at which bumping molecules move heat out of a building, insulation (a poor conductor of heat) is placed in walls, ceilings, and floors. Some common types of insulation are mineral wool, chopped paper, expanded polyurethane, and expanded polystyrene. Wood, concrete, brick, and glass are poor insulators.

Insulating materials are filled with small air spaces. Air is a poor conductor of heat because its molecules are relatively far apart. As a result, air molecules collide less often than solid and liquid molecules that touch one another. An insulator's many tiny air spaces greatly reduce the flow of heat to the cold air outside. It is similar to the thermal jacket you may wear in cold weather to keep you warm.

For a fixed heat source, how do you think insulation will affect the temperature difference between air inside and outside a building? Make a hypothesis. Then do this experiment.

1. Find a cardboard box about 30 centimeters (12 in) on a side. Place a socket with a 15-watt incandescent lightbulb inside the box at its center. Run its cord out of the box. Then seal the box with tape. (See Figure 9a.)

2. Use a digital or alcohol-based household thermometer to find the air temperature outside the box. Record that temperature.

3. Use a large nail to make a hole through one side of the box. Then carefully insert a laboratory thermometer through the hole. You can now measure the temperature inside the box.

4. Let the box represent a building with very little insulation. Plug the lightbulb into a wall socket and record the air temperature inside the "building" every 10 minutes. At what point does the temperature remain constant (stop increasing)? What must be true about the heat lost and the heat produced at this final temperature?

5. Now let's insulate the "building." First, remove the thermometer. Then place the cardboard box inside a large insulated box, such as the kind used to ship frozen foods. The insulated box should be only slightly larger than the cardboard box.

   If you don't have an insulated box, you can insulate the cardboard box yourself. Tie sheets of rigid-board insulation around the cardboard box. Be sure to wear gloves while handling insulation. You now have an insulated "building" (Figure 9b).

6. Use the large nail to make a hole through the insulation and the cardboard. Then insert the thermometer through the holes. Now you can measure the temperature inside the cardboard box.

# Figure 9

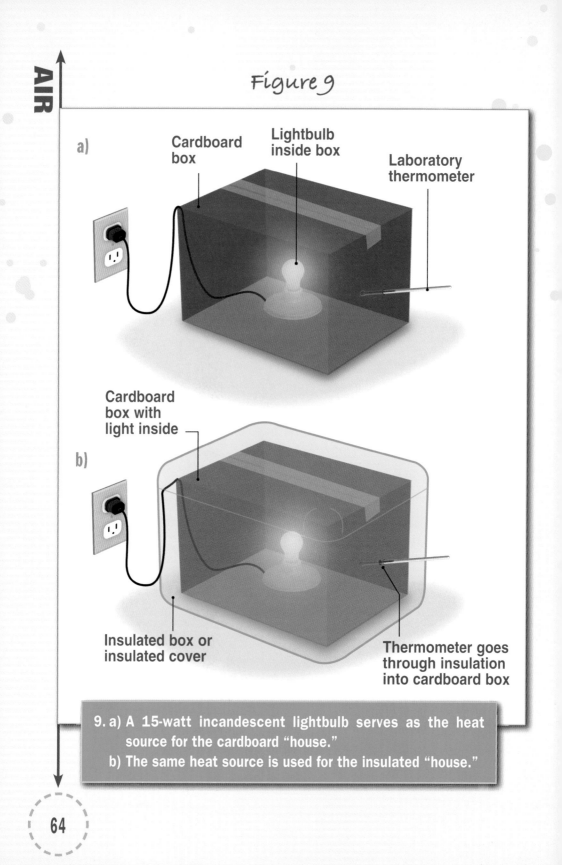

**a)**

Cardboard box

Lightbulb inside box

Laboratory thermometer

**b)**

Cardboard box with light inside

Insulated box or insulated cover

Thermometer goes through insulation into cardboard box

9. a) A **15-watt** incandescent lightbulb serves as the heat source for the cardboard "house."

   b) The same heat source is used for the insulated "house."

**7.** Plug the lightbulb into a wall socket and record the air temperature inside the "building" every 10 minutes. At what point does the temperature stop rising and remain constant? What must be true about heat lost and heat produced at this final temperature? How has the insulation affected the temperature difference between inside and outside air for a fixed heat source? Was your hypothesis correct?

## Ideas for Science Fair Projects

- Design experiments to test a variety of insulating materials, such as mineral wool batts, fiberglass batts, cellulose, and rigid board insulation. Which insulation best reduces heat losses?

- Does doubling the thickness of an insulator halve the rate of heat loss? Design an experiment to find out.

# Insulation and R-Values

Anything that reduces the flow (conduction) of heat is an insulator. Even an air space or an air film is an insulator because heat moves slowly through still air. Many older homes were not well insulated when fuel, usually wood or coal, was inexpensive. Most modern homes are heated by oil, gas, or electricity, which is expensive. Therefore, insulation is a necessity.

A material's ability to resist the flow of heat is known as its R-value. The larger a material's R-value, the better its ability to reduce the flow of heat. Table 2 lists some insulating materials and their R-values for given thicknesses.

To understand how insulation reduces the cost of heating a building, consider the R-values for an insulated and an uninsulated wall. An insulated wall is shown in Figure 10, and the R-values for insulated and uninsulated walls are shown on page 69. Compare the two R-values. They show that heat can move through the uninsulated wall almost four times faster than through the insulated wall. The comparison also shows that materials such as wood and wallboard offer some minimal insulation.

Because warm air is less dense than cold air, it tends to rise toward ceilings unless fans circulate the air. (The movement of fluids caused by a difference in density is called convection.) It is important that ceilings be well insulated. For buildings in the southern United States, the recommended insulation for attics above ceilings is R-19. R-38 is recommended for homes in the central part of the country. For buildings in northern cities, such as Helena, Montana, and

Duluth, Minnesota, the recommended R-value is 49, which is about 33 centimeters (13 in) of cellulose or 40.6 centimeters (16 in) of mineral wool batts.

## Table 2:
### R-Values of Some Common Insulating Materials

| Material | Thickness (inches) | R-Value |
|---|---|---|
| Mineral wool batt | 3.5 | 10.9 |
| Mineral wool batt | 6.0 | 18.8 |
| Expanded polyurethane | 1.0 | 5.9 |
| Expanded polystyrene | 1.0 | 4.2 |
| Air space | 3.5 | 1.0 |
| Glass | 0.125 | 0.9 |
| Cellulose fiber (paper) | 1.0 | 3.7 |
| Mineral wool | 1.0 | 4.0 |
| Sawdust | 1.0 | 2.2 |

## Figure 10

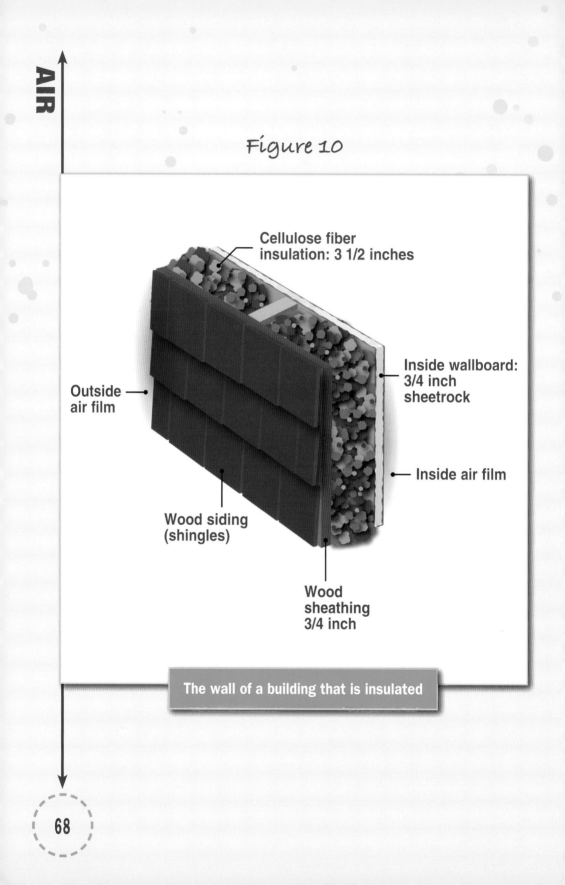

Cellulose fiber insulation: 3 1/2 inches

Inside wallboard: 3/4 inch sheetrock

Outside air film

Inside air film

Wood siding (shingles)

Wood sheathing 3/4 inch

**The wall of a building that is insulated**

| Wall Part | Insulated | R-value Uninsulated |
|---|---|---|
| Outside film of air | 0.2 | 0.2 |
| Wood siding | 0.8 | 0.8 |
| 0.5 in wood sheathing | 1.3 | 1.3 |
| 3.5 in air space | — | 1.0 |
| 3.5 in loose cellulose fiber | 13.0 | — |
| 0.5 in wall board (gypsum board) | 0.5 | 0.5 |
| Inside air film | 0.7 | 0.7 |
| Total R-value | 16.5 | 4.5 |

# 2.5 Finding Air Leaks
## (A Measurement)

**W**arm air can leave and cold air can enter through cracks in a building's surface. The most common places to find these air leaks, which can add greatly to heating costs, are around windows and doors. Such leaks cause what is called air infiltration. You can make a simple instrument—a moving air detector—to locate air leaks.

1. Cut a strip of plastic wrap about 15 centimeters x 8 centimeters (6 in x 3 in).

2. Tape a narrow end of the strip to a pencil.

3. Let the plastic wrap hang from the pencil. Gently blow on the device. What happens when moving air hits the strip?

4. On a windy day, use the instrument to search for air infiltration. Hold the instrument near closed, exterior windows and doors in your home. Also check in the basement around the foundation. Can you detect infiltration?

   Make a list of places where you find infiltration.

5. If you find places where air is infiltrating your home, tell your parents. Suggest that they buy weather stripping or caulking to seal these openings. Weather stripping and

caulk are inexpensive. But they can greatly reduce heat losses and heating bills.

6. Take your infiltration-detecting instrument to school and look for infiltrating air. Discuss your findings with your science teacher, custodian, or principal.

## Cooling Air With Trees

One way to reduce the cost of cooling your home in the summer is to plant deciduous trees on the south side of your house. The trees may eliminate or reduce the need for air conditioning. Their shade will block summer sun. But in the winter, the leafless trees will allow sunlight to pass through south-facing windows and warm the air inside your home. Trees can reduce the air temperature around your house by as much as 5°C (9°F). Window awnings can also reduce temperatures in your home by blocking sunlight.

## Green Buildings

In an effort to make Earth's air greener and reduce global warming, architects and builders are designing and erecting green buildings. Green buildings give us better air. They do so because they require less energy. They use less heat and electricity. Using less energy means fewer fossil fuels will be burned. Therefore, less carbon dioxide and less pollution will enter the air.

Building green includes the following materials and techniques, as well as others: (1) Using wallboard (the material that covers walls) made by companies that recycle materials. One such firm is CleanBoard, a California company. It uses recycled paper and the

In winter, sunlight can pass between the branches of the deciduous trees and help to warm the house.

In summer, the leafy trees shade the house helping to keep it cool.

ashes from coal-burning power plants to make wallboard in its solar-powered factory. (2) Reducing water use by: (a) Installing a system that captures gray water, such as bath water, and rainwater for irrigation. (b) Installing dual flush toilets that have a two-button system. One button provides a half-flush (3 liters) for liquid waste. A second button causes a full flush (6 liters) for solid waste. Conventional toilets use 19 liters per flush. (c) Providing men's rooms with urinals that require no water. (3) Reducing energy use by: (a) Using natural light and, where needed, compact fluorescent lightbulbs. (b) Installing automatic controls that turn off lights when people are not present. (c) Using E glass in windows. E glass reduces heat flow. It helps keep heat out in the summer and in during the winter. (d) Insulating walls, floors, and ceilings to reduce heating and cooling costs. (4) Conserving natural materials and reducing illness by: (a) Using interior paints, adhesives, and carpets that contain no hazardous chemicals. (b) Building with recycled materials. (c) Using only wood harvested from forests where any trees cut are replaced by planting new ones.

The roofs of green buildings are often covered with solar panels or solar collectors that provide clean electrical energy or heat. Heating systems are 95 percent efficient (only five percent of the heat goes up the chimney). Thermostats can be programmed to reduce the cost of heating the building by setting temperature to be warm when people are at home and cooler when they are away or asleep. Windows and doorframes are foam-sealed to prevent air from infiltrating. Where possible, much of the construction is done using recycled materials. Windows and appliances in green buildings are energy efficient. Outside these buildings, plants are used to reduce water use and control soil erosion. Permeable surfaces, such as gravel, allow water to seep into the soil where it can be absorbed by plants or added to the aquifer. Permeable paving is used in driveways and walks to reduce storm water run-off.

Many new, greener homes are built with 2-inch x 6-inch walls instead of the conventional 2-inch x 4-inch walls. The wider walls, when insulted, provide an R-value 1.5 times larger than the narrower 2-inch x 4-inch walls.

By using 2-inch x 6-inch framing boards instead of 2-inch x 4-inch boards (shown), thicker insulation can be placed in walls. The thicker insulation reduces heat losses.

# An Example of a Green Building

Thousands of green construction projects are planned. Many hope to be certified for LEED (Leadership in Energy and Environmental Design) and have registered with the U.S. Green Building Council. One example of a large green building is the California Academy of Sciences Museum in San Francisco. Its roof is green in more ways than one. It is covered with native species of green plants that absorb carbon dioxide and require no irrigation. In addition, thousands of solar cells line the roof overhangs and produce electricity. The building has no central air conditioning because when its windows are opened, winds off the Pacific Ocean serve as a natural means of cooling; recycled denim jeans are used for insulation. Inside, electronic sensors brighten or dim the lights depending on the amount of natural light entering the building.

# Rain Forests and Global Warming

Each year, large areas of forests in Brazil, Indonesia, and other countries are cut down and burned to make way for commercial or agricultural use. This clear cutting removes about 12 million hectares (30 million acres) of rain forests from Earth's surface. Clear cutting destroys ecosystems where plants and animals live. It also adds to global warming because trees remove carbon dioxide from the atmosphere. Carbon dioxide is a greenhouse gas, which traps heat in Earth's atmosphere and adds to global warming.

The green plants on this roof absorb carbon dioxide and reduce water runoff. (They may also provide vegetables during the growing season.)

Rain forests store nearly 30 percent of the world's carbon in their trees and other vegetation. In addition, rain forests contain half of Earth's known animal species, and more than 350 different ethnic groups. Seventy percent of the world's plants that have known medicinal value are located in these forests, so the destruction of rain forests also hinders medical progress.

As Table 3 reveals, deforestation, mostly due to the destruction of rain forests, is a major contributor to carbon dioxide in the air. If the trees had not been cut down, 5.43 billion tons of carbon dioxide would have been removed from the air.

| Table 3: Major Additions of Carbon Dioxide to the World's Air in 2008 (billions of tons) | |
|---|---|
| China      6.89 | European Union  5.07 |
| USA        6.73 | India        2.24 |
| Deforestation (worldwide)   5.43 | |

## Kids Go Green

Two fifth graders in Wilton, Connecticut, created an organization called "Little People, Big Changes." They talk to student groups and provide green information stations at libraries and supermarkets. Their efforts helped 200 households obtain electricity from renewable sources, such as wind, solar, and hydroelectric, even though it cost more. They fostered an anti-idling campaign to encourage drivers to not leave their car and truck motors running when they are not driving. Idling gasoline engines add pollutants to the air that create health risks.

Students at schools in Austin and Houston, Texas, have also promoted anti-idling campaigns. There are many more students throughout the country who are promoting a greener world. Perhaps you and your friends can help your community think and act green.

## Green Tips for Better Air

- If you have ceiling fans, set them to run counterclockwise in the summer. This will direct air downward, creating a breeze that will make you feel cooler. In the winter, run the fans clockwise to circulate air. Otherwise, the less dense warm air will rise to the ceiling and remain there, while colder, denser air will remain on the floor. Using ceiling fans correctly can reduce air conditioning costs by as much as 40 percent and heating bills by 10 percent.

- Improve air quality by conserving energy. Conserving energy will reduce air pollution produced by power companies that burn fossil fuels. Turn off lights not in use. Replace incandescent lightbulbs with compact fluorescent bulbs. Turn down thermostats at night and when away. Buy only energy efficient appliances (those with the Energy Star label). Turn off computers and other electronic devices when not in use. Dry clothes on a line in fresh air; clothes

dryers use a lot of electrical energy. Weatherize and insulate your home. Obtain an energy audit of your home; many power companies offer free audits.

- Plant trees. They remove carbon dioxide from air and provide summer shade.

- Check for air leakage from your refrigerator. Place a dollar bill between the gasket that seals your refrigerator door and the door itself. Close the door and pull on the bill. You should feel some resistance. If not, the door is leaking cold air that has to be replaced, causing the appliance to run more frequently and require more electrical energy.

- Caulk cracked, loose, or warped window frames and sills to prevent warm air from escaping and cold air from entering your living space.

- Special insulating covers are available for electrical outlets. They will stop cold air from entering your home's interior space.

- Replace furnace filters monthly to ensure efficiency and keep the air clean.

- Use the sun to heat inside air. Open drapes on south-facing windows. Close drapes at night to insulate windows.

- Remove mesh screens on south-facing windows in the winter. This will allow more solar energy to warm inside air.

- If your home has single-pane windows, add storm windows. This will reduce heat losses through windows to cold air by 50 percent.

- If you have a fireplace, be sure the damper is closed when not in use. Otherwise, warm air will be lost up the chimney.

- Turn off kitchen and bathroom-ventilating fans when not needed. These fans pull warm air to the outside. That lost air is replaced by cold outside air that must be heated.

# Our Polluted Air

When we talk about the great outdoors, we think of clear, open spaces and fresh air. However, that air is often polluted with dust, soot, ash, carbon monoxide, metal vapors, tiny sulfur dioxide droplets, and acidic raindrops. This pollution comes from factories, motor vehicles, power plants, forest fires, volcanoes, and other sources. Whenever fossil fuels are burned, particles of soot are emitted as well as chemical pollutants, such as carbon monoxide, carbon dioxide, and oxides of nitrogen and sulfur. When we breathe polluted air, its contents enter our lungs and possibly our bloodstream. The pollutants can cause serious illnesses, such as asthma, heart and lung diseases, cancer, and nerve disorders.

# 3.1 Capturing Polluting Particles in Air
## (An Experiment)

Things **YOU** will **Need:**

✓ paper punch
✓ 3 inch x 5 inch index cards
✓ clear, wide tape
✓ thread or rubber bands
✓ strong magnifying glass or microscope
✓ photograph in Figure 12

**Hypothesis: If there are particles polluting our air, we should be able to detect them.**

In this experiment, you will try to collect polluting particles. (Do not do this experiment immediately after a rainstorm. Rain cleanses the air of pollutants.)

1. Use a paper punch to make four holes along one edge of a 3-inch x 5-inch index card, as shown in Figure 11a. Make a fifth hole on one end of the card.

2. Place a piece of clear, wide tape over the first four holes (Figure 11b).

3. Make five more cards like this.

4. Use thread or rubber bands to hang the cards in different places inside and outside your home (Figure 11c). Inside, try hanging a card in your kitchen, bathroom, and basement. Outside, try hanging the cards from trees or posts near the road, your house, and in an open space.

# Figure 11

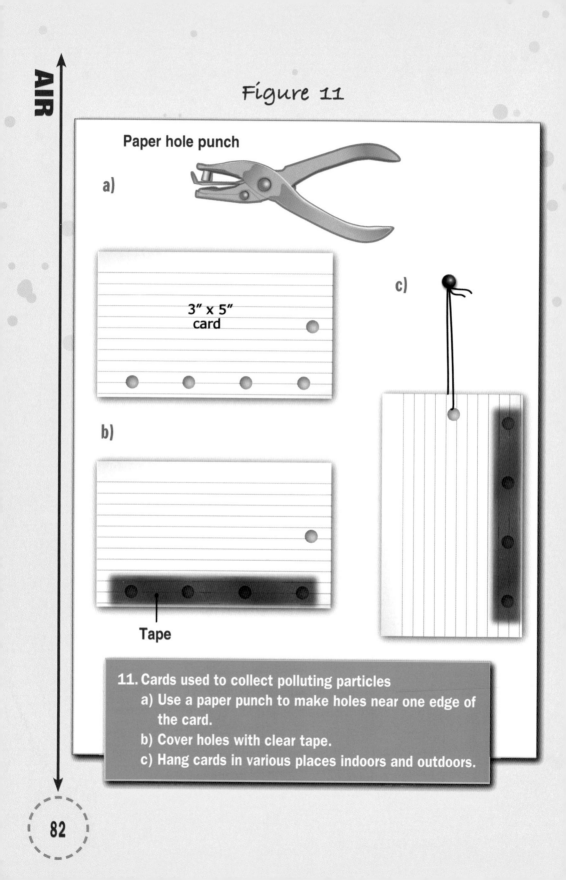

Paper hole punch

a)

3" x 5"
card

b)

Tape

c)

11. Cards used to collect polluting particles
   a) Use a paper punch to make holes near one edge of the card.
   b) Cover holes with clear tape.
   c) Hang cards in various places indoors and outdoors.

5. Leave the cards for about one week. If rain is forecast, bring the outdoor cards inside until it clears.

6. Collect the cards. Examine the sticky side of the tape over the holes with a strong magnifying glass or a microscope. As a control, for comparison with the exposed cards, make a new card and examine it immediately. It should have few, if any, particles on it.

7. Compare the particles you see on the exposed tape with the photograph in Figure 12. It shows a number of different particles often found in air. Can you identify any of the particles on your tapes?

## Figure 12

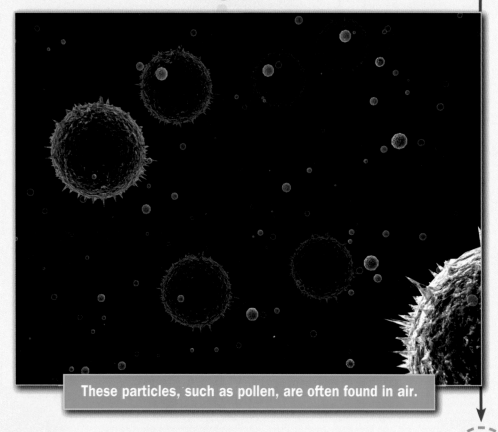

**These particles, such as pollen, are often found in air.**

## Idea for a Science Fair Project

Repeat Experiment 3.1, but this time coat a few microscope slides with a thin layer of petroleum jelly. Use another slide to spread the gooey stuff into a thin film on each slide. Put each slide on a thin piece of wood, such as a shingle. Use thumbtacks to hold the slides in place. Put the slides in various places.

After several days, collect the slides. Place cover slips on several regions of each slide. Use a microscope to examine the material under each cover slip. Can you see pollutants? Can you identify them? Where did you find the most pollution? The least pollution?

# Smog

Air pollution is found in many cities in the form of smog. Smog is a combination of smoke and fog. It may include a variety of chemical pollutants and particles. During an exceptionally cold December in 1952, thick, dark smog hung over London, England. It was a mix of coal smoke and fog. Londoners were used to smog, but the thick smog nearly shut down the city for five days. It was not until the smog lifted that anyone knew just how deadly the smog had been. Twelve thousand people died from breathing the polluted air. Thousands more were made sick by the unhealthful air. It led Great Britain to enact laws to reduce air pollution.

A thick haze of smog hangs over Los Angeles, California, at sunset.

Prolonged smog, such as the 1952 London smog, is caused by a temperature inversion. Normally, the temperature decreases about 6.5°C per kilometer of altitude (3.7°F/1,000 ft). But, if there is no wind to move air, a layer of cold air may become trapped below warmer air. Because cold air is denser than warm air, it tends to remain beneath the warmer air. The cold air can stay in place for a long time unless there is a wind to move it.

You can build a model to show how a cold air mass can remain trapped under a warm air mass.

# 3.2 A Trapped Cold Air Mass (A Model)

Things YOU Will Need:

✓ green food coloring
✓ 5 plastic medicine cups
✓ freezer
✓ water
✓ clear, glass pan about 8 inches x 5 inches x 3 inches deep

**W**ater and air are both fluids. You can use warm and cold water to represent warm and cold air.

1. Prepare five green ice cubes. Place two drops of green food coloring in each of five plastic medicine cups. Then fill the cups with water.

2. Place the cups in a freezer until the water is frozen.

3. When the green ice is available, nearly fill a clear, glass pan, such as the kind used to cook meat loaf, with water at room temperature.

4. The clear water in the pan represents warm air. Once the water stops moving, remove the green ice cubes from their cups. Place them in the water at one end of the pan. What happens as the ice melts?

5. After the green ice has melted, you will see a green layer of water under the clear water. The green water represents a cold air mass trapped beneath a warm air mass.

# 3.3 Making Smog
## (A Demonstration)

1. Find a tall glass jar. Fill it with cold water and a few ice cubes.

2. Cut a square of aluminum foil that is wider than the mouth of the jar.

3. Put some ice cubes on the foil. Set aside.

4. Empty the water from the jar, but leave one or two ice cubes. The air in the jar will now be cold and damp.

5. **Ask an adult** to light a small piece of paper and drop it into the jar of cold, damp air.

6. As soon as the flame goes out, have **the adult** cover the mouth of the jar with the aluminum foil and ice cubes.

7. Fold the foil over the top of the jar. Hold the foil in place with a rubber band. Watch what happens in the jar as the cold, damp air (fog) and smoke combine to make smog. What does the smog look like?

## Photochemical Smog

Another type of smog is photochemical smog, sometimes called Los Angeles smog. Unlike London smog, which peaks in the morning, photochemical smog peaks in the afternoon and is worst when bathed by warm sunshine. Also, unlike a London fog, it is first detected as an eye irritant, although it can cause lung damage as well. The irritating pollutant in this smog is ozone ($O_3$), a form of oxygen.

High in the stratosphere, ozone forms a protective layer that absorbs ultraviolet light from the sun. Ultraviolet light can damage living cells and cause skin cancer. While ozone in the stratosphere helps to protect us from ultraviolet rays, ozone on the ground is a harmful air pollutant.

Ozone is formed in strong sunlight when emissions from the exhaust pipes of motor vehicles combine chemically with air. A typical photochemical smog contains nitrogen oxides, carbon monoxide (CO), carbon dioxide ($CO_2$), hydrocarbons (compounds made of carbon and hydrogen), and various other organic compounds.

Photochemical smog is most common in large cities that enjoy a good deal of sunshine. But the smog can occur outside cities as well. Rural areas, particularly in the eastern United States, often experience ozone levels that exceed those in cities. High rural ozone levels are associated with high-pressure weather systems and heavy traffic.

Ozone is also produced when lightning travels through the oxygen in air. You can often smell the sharp odor of ozone following a thunderstorm. Wires carrying electricity to automobile spark plugs may produce small amounts of ozone. Over time, the ozone can cause the rubber coatings on such wires to deteriorate.

# 3.4 Air Pollution and Rubber (A Test and an Experiment)

- 2 metal coat hangers
- new, wide rubber bands
- shady place outdoors
- plastic bag that can be sealed
- twist tie
- dresser drawer
- magnifying glass

*Hypothesis: Ozone can cause rubber to deteriorate. Therefore, rubber bands in a region where ozone is a common pollutant should show signs of change when exposed to outside air. In a region where ozone is not a common air pollutant, rubber bands should exhibit little change over time.*

1. Bend two coat hangers to form two rectangles. Then stretch four new, wide rubber bands over each hanger (Figure 13a). Be sure the rubber bands are stretched. Bend the hangers some more if the rubber bands are not tight.

2. Hang one set of rubber bands outside in a shady place. Be sure that sunlight cannot reach the rubber. The ultra-violet light in sunlight can also cause rubber to change.

3. Place the other set of rubber bands in a completely sealed plastic bag (Figure 13b) so no additional air can reach it. Put this set of rubber bands in a closed dresser drawer.

# Figure 13

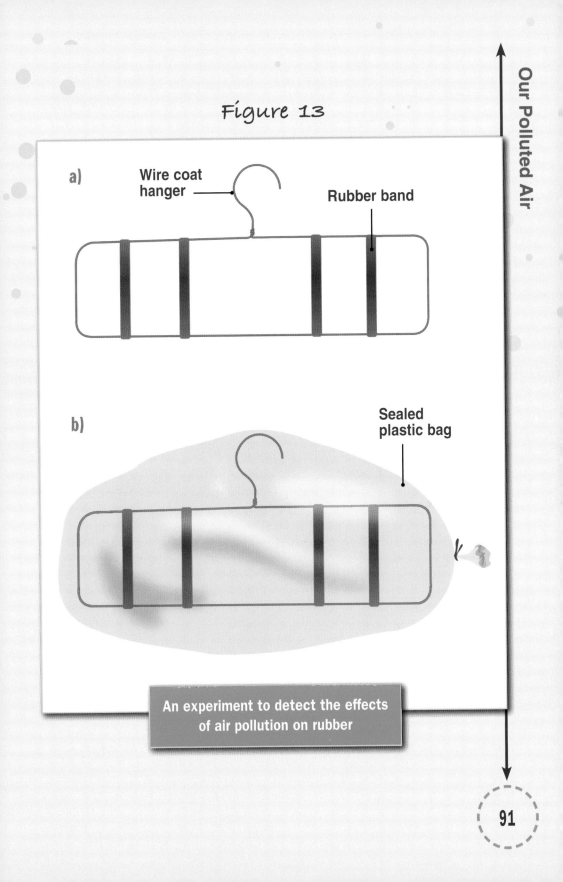

a)

Wire coat hanger

Rubber band

b)

Sealed plastic bag

An experiment to detect the effects of air pollution on rubber

4. After two weeks, examine the rubber bands that have been outdoors in what may be polluted air that contains ozone. Use a magnifying glass to examine them closely.

5. Compare the rubber bands you kept sealed inside a drawer with those you left outside. Stretch both sets of rubber bands the same distance. Do you observe any difference?

What are your results? Did you detect any changes in the rubber bands that hung in air? What, if anything, can you conclude?

**Idea for a Science Fair Project**

If you found evidence of ozone outside your home, do an experiment to see if there is ozone inside.

# 3.5 Acid Rain
## (A Measurement)

The atmosphere is mostly nitrogen (78%) and oxygen (21%). However, human industrial activities have polluted the air with other gases. Many of these gases, such as excess carbon dioxide ($CO_2$), sulfur dioxide ($SO_2$), and nitrogen dioxide ($NO_2$), dissolve in water found in the air. The dissolved gases combine with the water to form dilute carbonic acid ($H_2CO_3$), sulfuric acid ($H_2SO_4$), and nitric acid ($HNO_3$). The acidic moisture may form raindrops and fall to Earth as acid rain.

The strength of acids is measured in terms of pH. Neutral substances, such as pure water, have a pH of 7.0. Substances with a pH less than 7 are said to be acidic. Substances with a pH greater than 7 are alkaline, or basic.

Nearly all rain is slightly acidic. Rain with a pH as low as 5.6 is normal. Acid rain is defined as rain that has a pH less than 5.6. Acid rain can cause the pH of water in ponds, lakes, and streams to decrease. The water may become so acidic that it kills the eggs and seeds of some animals and plants.

1. Collect rain in plastic containers.

2. To measure the pH of the rain, use forceps to dip one end of a strip of pH test paper into the rainwater. Then compare the color of the test paper with a standard found on the container that holds the test paper. What is the pH of the rainwater you collected?

   If possible, use test paper that can measure pH to at least ±1/2 (0.5). That is, the paper should be able to distinguish pH 4.5 from pH 4.0 or pH 5.0. You may be able to borrow pH paper from your school. Or you can buy it from a science supply company (see Appendix) or a store that sells fish or swimming pool supplies.

## Ideas for Science Fair Projects

- Test the pH of rainwater at different times of the year. Does the pH of rain change from season to season?

- Is the pH of the rain at the beginning of a storm different than its pH near the end of the storm?

- Is the pH of rain affected by location? Is the rain in the eastern United States more acidic than the rain in the Midwest or the West Coast? You might exchange e-mail with students in other parts of the country who could measure the pH of rain where they live.

# Effects of Acid Rain

Many lakes are naturally alkaline, with a pH of 8. When acid rain causes the pH to fall to 7, concentrations of calcium in the water diminish. The eggs of some species of salamanders are so sensitive to the lower calcium concentrations that their populations begin to vanish.

At a pH of 6.6 snails die; at a pH of 6 tadpoles fail to mature. As the water becomes more acidic, more life forms die off. At a pH of 4.5, many fish die.

Acid rain falling on soil will dissolve chemical compounds containing mercury, cadmium, and lead, which are toxic. Many microorganisms essential for decomposing organic matter die when these toxic substances are present.

# 3.6 Does Rain Contain Salt? (An Experiment)

Gaseous pollutants in the air can make rain acidic. Do you think anything else might be dissolved in rain? How about salt? Could there be salt particles in the air where raindrops form? Make a hypothesis. Then do this experiment.

1. Find a clean, black plastic tray, such as the kind in which some frozen meals are sold.

2. Put the tray outside during a rainstorm so that rain will collect in the tray.

3. When it has stopped raining, bring the tray inside. Put it in a warm place where the rainwater will evaporate.

4. After the water has evaporated, look closely at the bottom of the tray. Is there any evidence that salt was dissolved in the rainwater? If so, what is the evidence?

# Condensation Nuclei and Raindrops

For raindrops to form, there must be particles called condensation nuclei. Water vapor in clouds condenses (changes from gas to liquid) on the particles. As you may have seen, rain may contain salt. Salt particles high in the atmosphere provide some of the condensation nuclei on which raindrops form. What other particles do you think might serve as condensation nuclei?

How can salt particles, which are solid, reach the altitudes where clouds are found?

When ocean waves break on beaches, the bubbles they carry burst, producing tiny salt-carrying droplets. These tiny droplets rapidly evaporate. The tiny salt particles that remain are carried upward by winds and updrafts into the atmosphere where they serve as condensation nuclei.

# Cars, Trucks, Pollution, and Generating Electricity With Air

As you learned in Chapter 3, the exhaust fumes from cars and trucks are major contributors to photochemical smog and air pollution. In this chapter, you will measure a car's fuel efficiency and see how fuel-efficient cars can improve air quality by reducing pollution. You will also investigate the effects of tire pressure and weight on fuel efficiency and see how air (wind) can be used to generate electrical energy without polluting the air.

# 4.1 Testing a Car for Fuel Efficiency
## (A Measurement)

Things YOU will Need:

- ✓ family car
- ✓ pen or pencil
- ✓ notebook
- ✓ pocket calculator (optional)

A car that can travel farther on one gallon of gasoline is more fuel-efficient than a car than travels fewer miles per gallon (mpg) of gasoline. The more fuel-efficient the car, the less pollution it is likely to add to the air. Car manufacturers are being required to produce cars with greater fuel efficiency. A more fuel-efficient fleet of cars on the road will lead to better air quality and reduce breathing disorders.

1. The next time your family's car needs fuel, be sure to get a full tank of gas. Then record the odometer reading (miles the car has traveled).

2. When the car next needs fuel, completely fill the tank again. Look at the readings on the gas pump. You will see the number of gallons that were required to fill the tank. Record the number of gallons. Also record the new odometer reading.

3. Use the two odometer numbers you have recorded to find the number of miles the car traveled between fueling. Divide the distance the car traveled by the number of

gallons needed to refill the tank. For example, suppose the odometer read 20,200.0 when the tank was first filled and 20,500.0 when it was refilled. If it took 10 gallons to refill the tank, then the car's fuel efficiency in miles per gallon (mpg) was:

$$\frac{20,500.0 - 20,200.0 \text{ mi}}{10 \text{ gal}} = \frac{300 \text{ mi}}{10 \text{ gal}} = 30 \text{ mpg}.$$

4. For better accuracy, continue to measure the car's fuel efficiency over several thousand miles. Take the average of these measurements. What is your family car's fuel efficiency in miles per gallon?

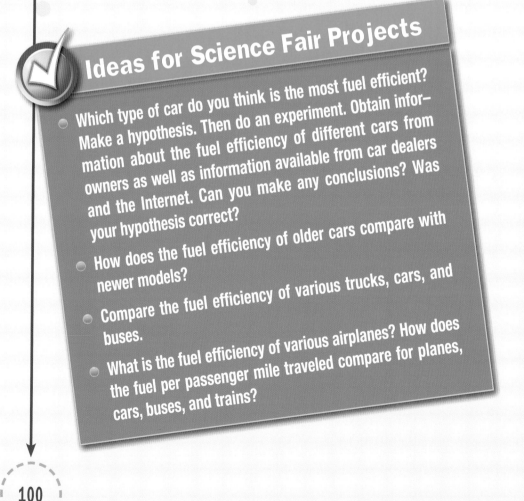

## Ideas for Science Fair Projects

- Which type of car do you think is the most fuel efficient? Make a hypothesis. Then do an experiment. Obtain information about the fuel efficiency of different cars from owners as well as information available from car dealers and the Internet. Can you make any conclusions? Was your hypothesis correct?

- How does the fuel efficiency of older cars compare with newer models?

- Compare the fuel efficiency of various trucks, cars, and buses.

- What is the fuel efficiency of various airplanes? How does the fuel per passenger mile traveled compare for planes, cars, buses, and trains?

# Fuel Efficiency Standards

New standards require new cars to average 35.5 mpg by 2016. The improved efficiency would add approximately $1,300 to the price of a new vehicle, but the improved efficiency would save more than $3,000 over the car's lifetime.

These standards will reduce greenhouse gas emissions by nearly 950 million metric tons per year while conserving 1.8 billion barrels of oil. It would be the equivalent of removing 42 million cars from our highways.

# 4.2 Friction and Tire Pressure
## (An Experiment)

**Things YOU will Need:**

- ✓ friend
- ✓ bicycle
- ✓ bicycle pump
- ✓ bicycle helmet
- ✓ spring scale
- ✓ smooth, level surface
- ✓ tire pressure gauge
- ✓ pen or pencil
- ✓ graph paper

**D**rivers are told to keep the tires of their cars inflated to a certain recommended pressure in order to obtain maximum fuel efficiency. Recognizing that an automobile has to overcome friction in order to move, how do you think low tire pressure will affect friction and, therefore, fuel efficiency? Form a hypothesis. Then do this experiment.

Friction is a force that acts against motion. If something moves at a constant speed along a level surface, the force making it move is equal to the force of friction opposing the motion. Applying a force greater than the frictional force will make the object accelerate (increase its speed).

1. Use a tire pressure gauge to check that your bicycle tires are inflated to the recommended pressure. Use a bicycle pump to add air if needed.

2. Ask a friend wearing a helmet to sit on your bicycle. Then use a spring scale (Figure 14a) to pull him or her along a smooth, level surface at a slow but steady speed. With what force do you have to pull the bike and your friend to overcome friction?

3. Let air out of the tires to reduce the pressure to about 4/5 of the recommended pressure. Then repeat the experiment.

4. Repeat the experiment at tire pressures of about 3/5, 2/5, and, finally, 1/5 of the original pressure. Does the frictional force acting on the bicycle change as the tire pressure decreases? How would low tire pressure affect the fuel efficiency of a car? How would it contribute to air quality?

5. Using the axes shown in Figure 14b, plot a graph of the frictional force on your bicycle versus the air pressure in the tires. What do you conclude? Was your hypothesis correct?

6. Use a bicycle pump to reinflate your tires to the proper pressure.

# Figure 14

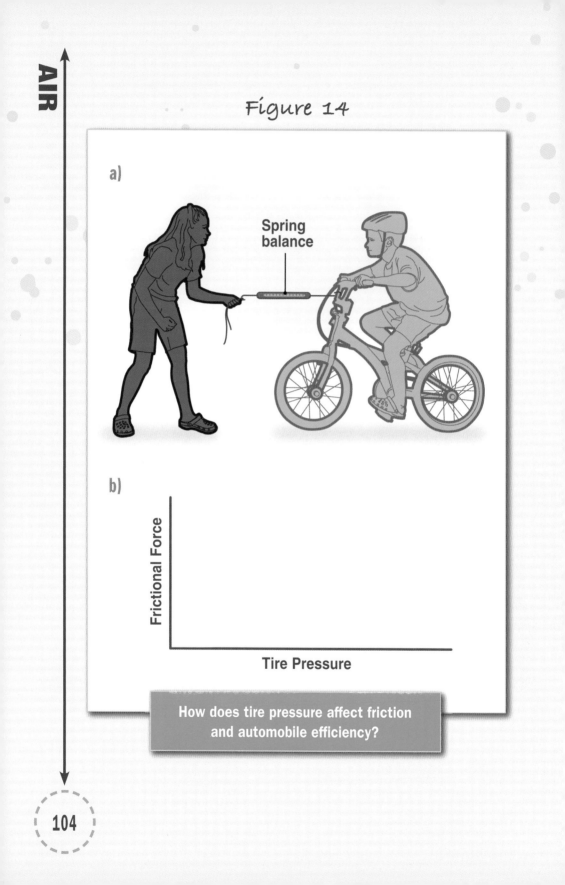

a)

Spring
balance

b)

Frictional Force

Tire Pressure

How does tire pressure affect friction
and automobile efficiency?

# Ideas for Science Fair Projects

○ Does the width of the tires affect the frictional force acting on the bicycle? Design and carry out an experiment to find out.

○ Does the diameter of the tires affect the frictional force acting on the bicycle? Design and carry out an experiment to find out.

○ In Experiment 4.2 you measured rolling friction. The wheel was free to turn as you pulled the bike along a level surface. Design and carry out an experiment to measure sliding friction—the force needed to slide the bicycle forward at a steady speed when the wheels can't turn. How does sliding friction compare with rolling friction?

○ Repeat Experiment 4.2 with the bike on different level surfaces. You might try it on blacktop pavement, concrete, dirt, gravel, grass, sand, and other surfaces. Is the frictional force that acts on your bicycle related to the surface over which the bike rolls? If it is, on which surface is the friction greatest? On which surface is friction the least?

# 4.3 Friction and Weight
## (An Experiment)

**Things YOU will Need:**
- ✓ people of different weights
- ✓ bicycle
- ✓ bicycle helmet
- ✓ spring scale
- ✓ smooth, level surface

**D**o you think a car's weight will affect its fuel efficiency? Form a hypothesis. Then carry out this experiment.

1. Have a friend who is not heavy put on a helmet and sit on your bike. Use a spring scale to pull the bike along a smooth, level surface at a slow but constant speed. What force is needed to do this?

2. Repeat this experiment with someone who is much heavier than the first person. Again, pull the bike with a spring scale along the same smooth, level surface at a slow but constant speed. What force was needed this time?

Did weight affect the friction between the bike and the surface over which it rolled? Was friction the same, greater, or less than it was when the lighter person was on the bike?

How would adding weight to a car affect its fuel efficiency? How would it affect air quality?

Was your hypothesis correct?

Why must you do this experiment on the same surface you used when you pulled the first person?

3. Repeat this experiment with someone who weighs much less than your first friend. Do you think the friction between the bike and the surface over which it rolls will be the same, greater, or less than it was when your first friend was on the bike? Try it. Were you right?

## Bicycles Don't Pollute

Riding a bicycle is healthier than riding in a car. People who ride bikes instead of driving cars help to reduce air pollution as well as America's dependence on foreign oil. Many cities, such as Columbia, Missouri, are building bike paths along city streets to make biking safer. Portland, Oregon, has spent nearly $60 million since 1992 to build new bike paths. It has bike routes throughout the city. As a result, car traffic has been greatly reduced. By using their cars less often, it is estimated that the average Portland biking family saves $2,500 per year. Portland is also one of a few U.S. cities to decrease its greenhouse gas emissions below their 1990 level.

In Davis, California, there are more bikes than cars. Tucson, Arizona, requires that all new streets include bike lanes, and in Boulder, Colorado, more than 90 percent of all major roads have bike lanes or paths. The city has also established safe routes to school to encourage students to bike or walk to school.

What can you do to encourage your city or town to promote biking? You and your fellow citizens will breathe better if you bike.

# Will Electric Cars Make a Comeback?

In 1900, most cars were powered by batteries. Then Henry Ford produced his Model T, which was powered by gasoline. It was less expensive, faster, and could travel farther than any electric car before refueling. Electric cars quickly faded from the roads.

Today, hybrid cars, powered by both gasoline and batteries, have improved automobile fuel efficiency while reducing polluting emissions. To further reduce gasoline consumption, air pollution, and America's dependence on foreign oil, almost every major automaker is developing an electric car.

For electric cars to be successful, the batteries must be able to power a car for long distances and provide reasonable acceleration. Most companies plan to use lithium-ion batteries, like the ones used in laptop computers and cell phones, only bigger. However, these batteries are expensive and if overheated or overcharged, they can catch fire.

Engineers are working to make the batteries smaller, safer, and more efficient. There are also plans to develop fuel stations where discharged batteries could be replaced with ones that are fully charged. Alternatively, batteries might be made to recharge quickly. Then there could be stations where cars could be plugged in and recharged within a few minutes.

Of course, the energy to recharge these plug-in electric cars will come from power plants. So we would need more electric power. To become a truly green nation, the electricity should come from

During rush hour, thousands of cars hit the roads in cities across the United States.

renewable sources of energy, such as solar, wind, and water (hydroelectric).

# Carpooling

In 2005, the Texas Transportation Institute investigated traffic jams. They found congested traffic causes 3.7 billion hours of delay each year in the United States. It wastes 2.3 billion gallons of gasoline, and adds to air pollution. Carpooling can reduce traffic congestion, make our air cleaner, conserve energy, and reduce our use of fossil fuels. By sharing a vehicle, people can save money, reduce air pollution and personal distress, and have a chance to relax or read while riding to work.

In 2005, only 10.7 percent of commuters took a car pool to work. What can you do to encourage people to carpool?

# Drive and Travel Green

To increase fuel efficiency, reduce air pollution, and save money, drivers should obey speed limits, not rev engines, and accelerate and brake gradually. Fuel consumption and polluting emissions are lowest at moderate speeds, accelerations, and braking. Drivers should avoid heavy holiday traffic where backups are common. A car sitting in traffic consumes much more gasoline and emits more pollution than one at cruising speed. By avoiding holiday traffic, most traffic tie-ups and the frustration they cause can be avoided. If possible, travel in a hybrid car. Hybrids consume much less fuel and emit far less carbon dioxide and other pollutants.

If you fly, fly green. Buy a nonstop, coach ticket. First class seats occupy more space and, therefore, consume more fuel per passenger than do smaller coach seats. Nonstop flights use less fuel and emit less carbon emissions than those that make landings prior to the final destination. Landings and takeoffs are fuel gobblers.

You can also take the bus. It is the most efficient and least expensive means of travel. Two people traveling by bus generate considerably less carbon than if they were to fly or drive a car.

# 4.4 An Electric Motor as a Generator
## (A Demonstration)

**Things YOU will Need:**

- an adult
- small, electric motor (buy at an electronics store, hobby shop, toy store, or science supply company)
- 2 insulated wires with clips
- milliammeter or microammeter
- bicycle
- gloves
- 1.2-volt flashlight bulb
- bulb holder
- thick rubber or plastic tubing with a very small inside diameter

Moving air (wind) can be used to generate green electric energy. The giant blades on wind turbines turn electric generators in order to produce electrical energy without polluting the air.

A small, toy electric motor can be used to generate small amounts of electricity. These motors have one or more coils of wire that can turn between magnets. When connected to a battery, an electric current (moving electric charges) flows through the coils. The magnets push on the moving charges and make the coils turn.

This same motor can work as an electric generator. If you turn the coils yourself, the magnetic field through the coils will change and electric charges will be pushed along the wires.

1. Examine a small, toy electric motor. There should be two metal leads outside the case that encloses the motor. These leads are connected to the motor's coils. Use two insulated wires with alligator clips to connect the two leads to the poles of a milliammeter or a microammeter. (A milliammeter measures thousandths of an ampere. A microammeter measures millionths of an ampere.) Electric currents are measured in units called amperes.

2. Spin the motor's shaft with your fingers. Is an electric current generated? What happens if you turn the shaft faster? What happens if you spin it in the opposite direction? How can you explain what you see?

3. Turn a bicycle upside down. You can use the bicycle wheel as a turbine to turn the generator's coils. Give the front wheel a good spin. Hold the milliammeter or microammeter connected to the generator (electric motor) while **an adult**, wearing a glove, holds the generator's shaft against the spinning tire (Figure 15). Can an electric current be generated by using the spinning wheel to turn the generator's shaft?

4. Connect the generator's leads to a 1.2-volt flashlight bulb in a bulb holder. Again, **ask an adult**, wearing a glove, to hold the motor's shaft against the side of a spinning bike tire. Can enough current be generated to light the bulb?

5. You may have to increase the friction between the spinning tire and the generator's shaft to make the generator spin fast enough to light the bulb. To do this, slide thick rubber or plastic tubing over the shaft of the generator. The additional friction should enable you to light the 1.2-volt flashlight bulb.

## Figure 15

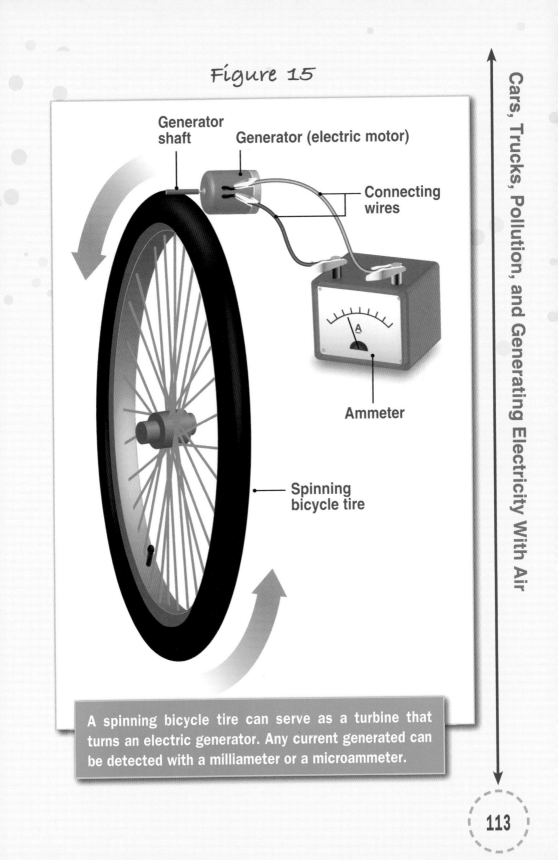

Generator shaft

Generator (electric motor)

Connecting wires

Ammeter

Spinning bicycle tire

A spinning bicycle tire can serve as a turbine that turns an electric generator. Any current generated can be detected with a milliameter or a microammeter.

## Ideas for Science Fair Projects

- Figure out a way to generate a steady electric current from your small motor-generator.

- Do an experiment to show how increasing the diameter of the generator's shaft affects its rate of rotation. Will it make the shaft spin faster or slower?

# 4.5 A Pinwheel Turbine: Generating Electricity With Air

## (A Model)

**Things You will Need:**

- ✓ an adult
- ✓ pinwheel
- ✓ small generator (motor) from Experiment 4.4
- ✓ wood dowels
- ✓ rubber or plastic tubing
- ✓ tape
- ✓ 2 wires with alligator clips
- ✓ milliammeter or microammeter
- ✓ electric fan

You can make a model wind turbine that uses moving air to generate electric energy. Using wind to generate electric energy is a clean way to provide electricity. No carbon dioxide or other pollutants are added to the air. It is a green way to go!

In the previous demonstration, you used a spinning bicycle tire as a turbine to turn a small generator. A toy pinwheel looks more like the blades of a wind turbine than a bicycle wheel. Can the pinwheel turn the small generator (motor) you used in 4.4? Let's find out.

1. Because pinwheels differ, you will have to figure out a way to connect the pinwheel's shaft to the generator shaft. With help from **an adult**, you may be able to use a wood dowel, rubber or plastic tubing, and tape to make the connection. One example using plastic tubing is shown in Figure 16a.

2. Use wires with alligator clips to connect the generator to a milliammeter or a microammeter. Use wind from a fast-spinning fan to turn the pinwheel turbine (Figure 16b).

Does the generator produce an electric current when turned by a "wind turbine"?

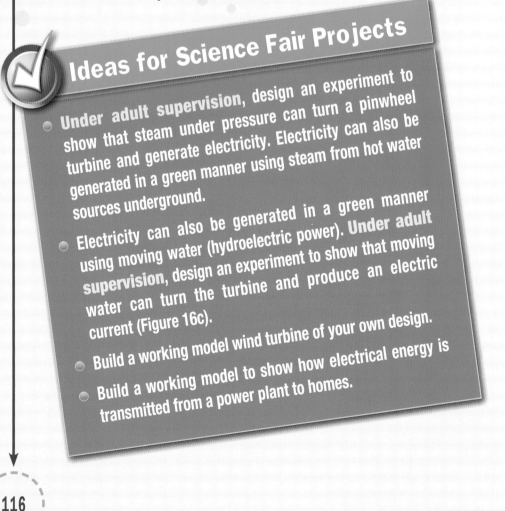

## Ideas for Science Fair Projects

- **Under adult supervision**, design an experiment to show that steam under pressure can turn a pinwheel turbine and generate electricity. Electricity can also be generated in a green manner using steam from hot water sources underground.

- Electricity can also be generated in a green manner using moving water (hydroelectric power). **Under adult supervision**, design an experiment to show that moving water can turn the turbine and produce an electric current (Figure 16c).

- Build a working model wind turbine of your own design.

- Build a working model to show how electrical energy is transmitted from a power plant to homes.

Figure 16

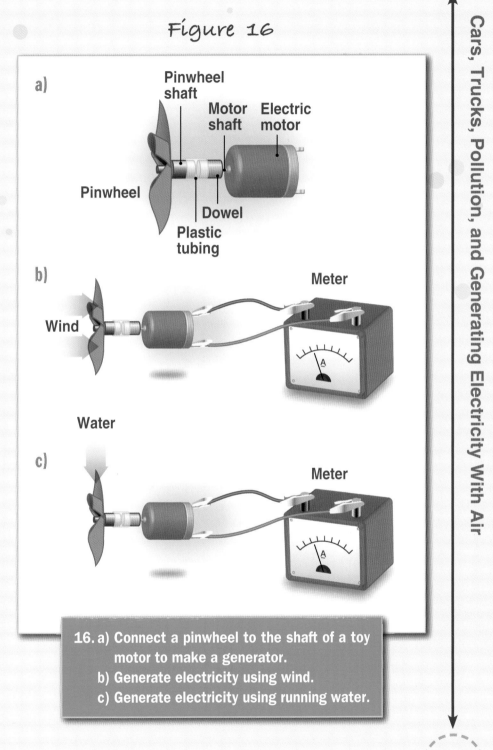

16. a) Connect a pinwheel to the shaft of a toy
    motor to make a generator.
    b) Generate electricity using wind.
    c) Generate electricity using running water.

# Greener Air for a Greener World

We live in a polluted sea of air on a planet that obtains most of its energy by burning fossil fuels. As a result, the increase of greenhouse gases in our air, particularly carbon dioxide, has led to global warming.

As Earth grows warmer, ancient land glaciers and Arctic ice are melting. Water from the glaciers flows into the ocean causing sea levels to rise, threatening islands and coastal cities with flooding. Loss of Arctic ice means less sunlight is reflected back into space so ocean waters absorb more heat. Warmer oceans provide more fuel for violent hurricanes. The change in ocean temperature may also cause ocean currents to shift, causing drastic changes in climates throughout the world. These and other effects lie ahead unless we act.

How we get our energy is the key to reducing global warming and improving our air quality. To reduce the amount of carbon dioxide entering our air, we need to convert to renewable sources of energy: solar, wind, hydroelectric, tidal, and geothermal. (Although not renewable, nuclear energy from uranium and plutonium does not produce any carbon dioxide or other greenhouse gases.)

The change to renewable energy sources is making progress. More people are installing solar panels on south-facing roofs. The number of wind turbines on windswept land is increasing as well. Also, more coastal areas are making plans to build these turbines in coastal waters as well.

But the switch to renewable energy will take time. In the meantime, scientists and engineers are developing the technology needed to bury large amounts of carbon dioxide deep within the earth. Burying the carbon dioxide will prevent it from entering the air and lessen global warming.

However, as individuals, there are things that we can do now to reduce global warming and improve air quality.

- Encourage people to drive cars less, walk and bike more, and use public transportation.

- When cars are needed, drive automobiles that are fuel-efficient, carpool, and avoid unnecessary mileage by combining trips, such as work and shopping.

- To reduce fuel consumption, encourage people to drive at reasonable speeds, avoid aggressive driving, keep cars tuned, tires properly inflated, and, when possible, work at home.

- Where possible, choose green electricity from wind, solar, hydroelectric, geothermal, tidal, wave, and nuclear sources even though the cost may be more.

- In your home, buy energy-efficient appliances, wash clothes in warm or cold water, install low flow shower heads and fluorescent lighting, set hot water heaters at 49°C (120°F), operate dishwashers only when they are full, lower thermostats at night and when you are away, apply for an energy audit, install solar panels on your roof, and do everything you can to reduce energy use.

- Buy from green businesses and encourage people to vote for candidates who favor green policies and green taxes.

Improve our air. Think green!

# Appendix:
# Science Supply Companies

**Arbor Scientific**
P.O. Box 2750
Ann Arbor, MI 48106-2750
(800) 367-6695
www.arborsci.com

**Carolina Biological Supply Co.**
2700 York Road
Burlington, NC 27215-3398
(800) 334-5551
http://www.carolina.com

**Connecticut Valley Biological
    Supply Co., Inc.**
82 Valley Road, Box 326
Southampton, MA 01073
(800) 628-7748
http://www.ctvalleybio.com

**Delta Education**
P.O. Box 3000
80 Northwest Blvd
Nashua, NH 03061-3000
(800) 258-1302
customerservice@delta-education.
    com

**Edmund Scientific's Scientifics**
60 Pearce Avenue
Tonawanda, NY 14150-6711
(800) 728-6999
http://www.scientificsonline.com

**Educational Innovations, Inc.**
362 Main Avenue
Norwalk, CT 06851
(888) 912-7474
http://www.teachersource.com

**Fisher Science Education**
4500 Turnberry Drive
Hanover Park, IL 60133
(800) 955-1177
http://www.fishersci.com

**Frey Scientific**
100 Paragon Parkway
Mansfield, OH 44903
(800) 225-3739
http://www.freyscientific.com

**Nasco-Fort Atkinson**
P.O. Box 901
Fort Atkinson, WI 53538-0901
(800) 558-9595
http://www.nascofa.com

**Nasco-Modesto**
P.O. Box 3837
Modesto, CA 95352-3837
(800) 558-9595
http://www.nascfao.com

**Sargent-Welch/VWR Scientific**
P.O. Box 5229
Buffalo Grove, IL 60089-5229
(800) SAR-GENT
http://www.SargentWelch.com

**Science Kit & Boreal Laboratories**
777 East Park Drive
P.O. Box 5003
Tonawanda, NY 14150
(800) 828-7777
http://sciencekit.com

**Wards Natural Science
    Establishment**
P.O. Box 92912
Rochester, NY 14692-9012
(800) 962-2660
http://www.wardsci.com

# Glossary

**acid rain**—Rain with a pH less than 5.6.

**air**—The gases that make up Earth's atmosphere, which are primarily nitrogen (78%) and oxygen (21%).

**air pollution**—Contaminants in the air, such as dust, soot, ash, carbon monoxide, metal vapors, tiny sulfur dioxide droplets, and acidic raindrops. This pollution comes from factories, motor vehicles, power plants, forest fires, volcanoes, and other sources.

**air pressure**—The pressure exerted by Earth's air, which can support a column of mercury 76 centimeters (29.9 in) high.

**aneroid barometer**—An instrument that uses an evacuated can to measure air pressure.

**barometer**—An instrument used to measure air pressure.

**carpooling**—When more than one person commutes to work or other activities in a single car. The driver shares his car with others.

**condensation nuclei**—Tiny particles, such as salt crystals, on which water vapor in clouds condenses to form raindrops.

**deciduous trees**—Trees that lose their leaves in winter.

**density**—The mass or weight of a substance divided by its volume.

**electric cars**—Cars powered by electrical energy.

**electrical generator**—A machine that produces electrical energy by turning coils of wire in a magnetic field.

**evaporation**—The change of a liquid into a gas as the liquid absorbs heat.

**friction**—A force that opposes motion.

**fuel efficiency**—The distance a motor vehicle can travel on one gallon of fuel.

**global warming**—The gradual warming of Earth due to an increase in greenhouse gases, such as carbon dioxide.

**greenhouse gases**—Atmospheric gases, such as carbon dioxide and methane, that reflect radiant heat energy back to Earth.

**hybrid cars**—Cars powered by both an internal combustion engine and a battery.

**infiltration**—The movement of air through openings in a building's exterior walls. This usually occurs around doors and windows that are not properly weather-stripped or caulked.

**insulation**—Materials that resist the conduction of heat.

**mercury barometer**—An instrument that measures air pressure by the height of a column of mercury supported by air.

**mesosphere**—A layer of Earth's atmosphere that extends from about 50 to 80 kilometers (31 to 50 mi) above Earth's surface.

**pH**—A measure of acidity. Acids have a pH less than 7; bases (alkalis) have a pH greater than 7. Substances with a pH of 7 are said to be neutral, neither acidic nor basic.

**photochemical smog**—A smog in which the major pollutant is ozone ($O_3$), a form of oxygen formed in strong sunlight when hydrocarbons and nitrogen oxides emitted from the exhaust pipes of motor vehicles combine chemically. In addition to these chemicals, a typical photochemical smog contains carbon monoxide (CO), carbon dioxide ($CO_2$), and other organic compounds.

**photovoltaic cells**—Devices that can convert light energy into electrical energy.

**pressure**—A force divided by the area on which the force pushes.

**R-value**—A measurement of an insulator's ability to resist the flow of heat. The greater the R-value, the greater the material's ability to resist heat conduction.

**smog**—A combination of smoke and fog, often found in cities where there is a temperature inversion.

**solar collectors**—Panels found on roofs that convert solar energy (sunlight) to heat.

**stratosphere**—A layer of Earth's atmosphere that extends from about 13 to 50 kilometers (8 to 31 mi) above Earth's surface.

**temperature**—A measurement of the average kinetic (motion) energy of molecules.

**temperature inversion**—A situation in which cold, dense air lies under warm, less dense air.

**thermosphere**—A layer of Earth's atmosphere that extends outward from about 80 kilometers (50 mi) to outer space.

**troposphere**—The lowest level of Earth's atmosphere. It extends from Earth's surface to a height of approximately 13 kilometers (8 mi).

# Further Reading

Bardhan-Quallen, Sudipta. *Championship Science Fair Projects: 100 Sure-to-Win Experiments.* New York: Sterling, 2007.

David, Sarah B. *Reducing Your Carbon Footprint at Home.* NewYork: The Rosen Publishing Group, Inc., 2009.

Gore, Al. *An Inconvenient Truth: The Crisis of Global Warming, revised edition.* Adapted for young readers by Jane O'Connor. New York: Viking, 2007.

McKay, Kim, and Jenny Bonnin. *True Green Kids: 100 Things You Can Do to Save the Planet.* Washington, D.C.: National Geographic Society, 2008.

Rhatigan, Joe, and Rain Newcomb. *Prize-Winning Science Fair Projects for Curious Kids.* New York: Lark Books, 2006.

Sechrist, Darren. *Air Pollution: What Is It? Why Is It Happening? Does It Matter?* Tarrytown, N.Y.: Marshall Cavendish Benchmark, 2009.

Sobha, Geeta. *Green Technology: Earth-Friendly Innovations.* New York: Crabtree Publishing Company, 2008.

Thornhill, Jan. *This Is My Planet: The Kids' Guide to Global Warming.* Toronto: Maple Tree Press, 2007.

Trask, Crissy. *It's Easy Being Green: A Handbook for Earth-Friendly Living.* Layton, Utah: Gibbs Smith, 2006.

Walker, Jane. *Atmosphere in Danger.* Mankato, Minn.: Stargazer Books, 2005.

# Internet Addresses

**Ecological Footprint**
http://myfootprint.org

**Footprint Calculator**
http://www.zerofootprintkids.com

**Green for All**
http://greenforall.org

**United States Environmental Protection Agency Student Center**
http://www.epa.gov/kids/air.htm

# Index